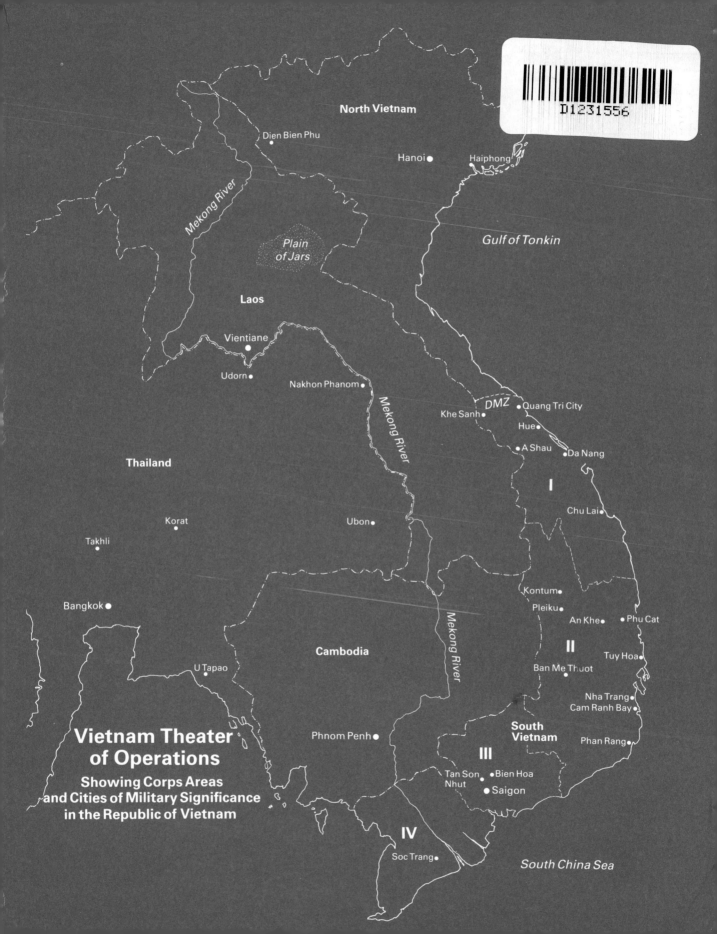

North Vietnam

Dien Bien Phu

Hanoi • • Haiphong

Mekong River

Gulf of Tonkin

Plain of Jars

Laos

Vientiane •

Udorn •

Nakhon Phanom •

Mekong River

DMZ

Khe Sanh • • Quang Tri City

Hue •

• A Shau • Da Nang

I

Thailand

Chu Lai •

Korat •

Ubon •

Takhli •

Kontum •

Pleiku •

An Khe • • Phu Cat

Bangkok •

Cambodia

Mekong River

II

Tuy Hoa •

Ban Me Thuot •

U Tapao •

Nha Trang •

Cam Ranh Bay •

Phnom Penh •

III

South Vietnam

Phan Rang •

Vietnam Theater of Operations

Showing Corps Areas and Cities of Military Significance in the Republic of Vietnam

Tan Son Nhut • • Bien Hoa

• Saigon

IV

Soc Trang •

South China Sea

UNIFORMS
OF THE
INDO~CHINA
AND
VIETNAM
WARS

UNIFORMS OF THE INDO~CHINA AND VIETNAM WARS

Leroy Thompson

Illustrated by
Michael Chappell,
Malcolm McGregor
and Ken MacSwan

BLANDFORD PRESS
POOLE · DORSET

For 'Bull Simons'
Chet Vinh Hon Song Nhuc

First published in the U.K. 1984 by Blandford
Press, Link House, West Street, Poole, Dorset,
BH15 1LL

Distributed in the United States by
Sterling Publishing Co., Inc.,
2 Park Avenue, New York, N.Y. 10016

British Library Cataloguing in Publication Data

Thompson, Leroy
 Uniforms of the Indo-China and Vietnam Wars.
 1. Vietnamese conflict, 1961-1975   2. Uniforms,
 Military—History—20th century
 I. Title   II. Chappell, Michael
 III. McGregor, Malcolm   IV. Turner, Pierre
 355.1'4'09597   UC485.V6

ISBN 0 7137 1264 3

Typeset in 10/11pt Monophoto Plantin by
August Filmsetting, Warrington, Cheshire.

Printed in Italy by New Interlitho S.P.A.

Frontispiece: USN SEAL in ambush along a Mekong Delta trail. He wears 'Tiger Stripes' camouflage with an OD head scarf. His camo face paint was typical of the SEALs. He has a Ka-Bar fighting utility knife and the 5.56 mm caliber M63A1 LMG favored by the SEALs. With the 150 round drum magazine as here, the M63A1 had a lot of firepower.

CONTENTS

Acknowledgements

Photograph credits (black and white/*colour*). Australian War Memorial: 136, 137, *138* (right), *139*. Courtney Phelps Collection: *52* (top), 54 (bottom), 149 (bottom right). Delayen: *18*. ECPA: 8, 9, 12, 16, 17, 20, 21, 22, 108, 123. Society of Vietnamese Rangers: 39. US Air Force: 85, *86*, *87*, 88, 89, *92*, *94*, *95*, 96, 97, 98, 99, 100, 101, *102*, 103, 104. US Army: 25, 29, *30*, 33, *34*, 37, 40, 44, 45, *46*, *47*, 48, 49, *50*, 51, 52 (bottom), 53, 54 (top), *55*, *119*, 125, 126, 128, 129, *131*, 132, 133, 134, *135*, 136 (lower), *138* (left). US Marine Corps: 57, 60, 61, 64, 65, 66, 67, 68, 69, 70, *71*, 72, 73, 74, 84, 109, 113, 114, 116, 117. US Navy: *2/3*, *75*, 76, *77*, 80, 81, *82*, *83*, *118*. Don Valentine/Larry Greene: 28. West Point Museum Collection: 145, 149 (top, center, bottom left), *153*.

Artwork credits Michael Chappell: *63*, *111*, *127*, *151*. Malcolm McGregor: *11*, *15*, *27*, *31*, *147*. Ken J. MacSwan: *43*, *79*, *91*, *107*.

The assistance of the above named, and of the U.S. Department of Defense Audiovisual Agency, Silver Image Ltd, and Robert Fisch, West Point Museum in compiling the illustrations for this book is gratefully acknowledged.

1 The French Indo-China War

At the end of World War II the 20th Indian Division from Admiral Mountbatten's Allied Southeast Asian Command was assigned the re-occupation of the southern part of Vietnam, and Chiang Kai-shek's Nationalist Chinese Forces were assigned the re-occupation of the northern part of Vietnam. Although some re-armed French troops who had been prisoners of the Japanese had begun to re-exert French authority in Saigon and other parts of southern Vietnam by September, 1945, it was not until February, 1946, that a French expeditionary force re-entered northern Vietnam. A major expeditionary corps under General Leclerc and composed of the 2nd Armored Division and the 3rd and 9th Colonial Infantry Divisions arrived at Saigon in October, 1945. Ho Chi Minh, however, had entered Hanoi in September, 1945, as a liberator and had declared a Democratic Republic of Vietnam.

During 1946 as the French tried to consolidate their control over northern Vietnam there were several armed clashes with the Viet Minh. During the re-entry of Haiphong on 6 March, in fact, French landing forces had even been fired on by the Nationalist Chinese. This same day France recognized the independence of Vietnam as a member of the French Union, but the Viet Minh did not accept this. On 23 November, 1946, the French naval bombardment of Haiphong by the sloop *Savorgnan de Brazza* as well as other ships resulted in 6000 civilian deaths, thus giving Ho Chi Minh a propaganda victory even though the French had regained control of the principal cities of northern Vietnam by the end of 1946. Ho Chi Minh and General Giap were still very active in the countryside though.

Among French troops already in Indo-China by the end of 1946 were the 2nd Foreign Legion Infantry Regiment (2 REI) which had landed in February and the 3rd Foreign Legion Infantry Regiment (3 REI) which had arrived between April and June. The 13th Foreign Legion Demi-Brigade (13 DBLE) had also landed in March, 1946. French naval airborne commandos (Commando Ponchardier) and a French SAS battalion had been in Indo-China since October, 1945, and continued to serve throughout most of 1946. In August, the Commando Ponchardier returned to France, but the SAS battalion remained in Vietnam. To patrol and secure the multitude of waterways a 3000 man naval brigade began operations in early 1946 as well. In addition colonial infantry and motorized infantry regiments – including some North African units – arrived in 1946.

In early 1947, Viet Minh forces besieged Hue, but by February French troops had lifted the siege. Throughout 1947 and 1948 the French tried to fight the Viet Minh using traditional methods such as pincer movements to surround the Communists. 'Operation Lea', in October, 1947, for example, involved the drop of 1137 paratroopers near the Viet Minh HQs at Bac Kan, Cho Moi, and Cho Don in an attempt to capture rebel leaders. An armored, infantry, and artillery column was also involved in this operation along with amphibious units. The Spitfire equipped 4th Fighter Group gave air support. Although important documents and many supply depots were captured in 'Lea', most Communist leaders escaped. By 8 November 'Lea' was over, with most Viet Minh troops having slipped through the net.

In 1947 and 1948 some of the French paras who were to earn such fame in Indo-China began to arrive. Among the parachute units deployed to Indo-China or formed there in 1947 and '48 were the 1st BCCP (Colonial Commando Parachute Battalion), 2nd BCCP, 5th BCCP, and the 1st RCP (Chasseurs Parachute Regiment). By the end of 1948, 40 combat jumps had already been made by French paras in Indo-China, too. The largest had been the one in 'Operation Lea', but two other operations – at Phu Tho in May, 1947, and at Day in December, 1948, had involved 1000 jumpers. The 1st Foreign Legion Parachute Battalion (1 BEP) arrived in November, 1948. The 1st CIP (Indo-Chinese Parachute Company) was also formed with Indo-Chinese personnel in 1948.

By the middle of 1949, French Union Forces in

A French colonial infantry unit being reviewed by Gen. Leclerc, early in the Indo-china War. Illustrating the assortments of uniforms and equipment worn by French forces. These men were equipped by the Australians, including 'digger' hats. Colonial infantry insignia is worn on the sleeves of the men in the right foreground.

Vietnam totaled nearly 150,000 men, but most of these were tied down to static defensive assignments. Much of the burden of carrying the war to the enemy offensively fell on the camo clad shoulders of the paras whose strength by 1950 would reach almost 5700 men. 1949 also saw the defeat of Nationalist Chinese forces by the Communist Chinese, giving Ho Chi Minh a powerful ally in the north. French killed and missing in action increased slightly in 1949 to 4872, up from 4821 in 1948 and 4081 in 1947.

Although Algerian and Moroccan troops as well as locally recruited Cambodian, Laotian, and Vietnamese units made up a goodly percentage of the nearly 150,000 troops in Vietnam during 1949, the most important new arrivals in that year were the 3rd BCCP, the 6th BCCP, and the 2nd BEP and the 5th REI.

As of January, 1950, Ho Chi Minh was recognized by the People's Republic of China as the 'true' leader of Vietnam, and supplies began

flowing at an increasing rate to the Viet Minh. During much of 1950 fighting was sporadic, but in September, General Giap's forces launched major assaults against French forts along the Chinese border. Beginning on 1 October these scattered forts manned by about 10,000 troops were attacked one by one. By 17 October all of the forts had fallen. Paras from the 1st BEP, 3rd BCCP, 3rd GCCP, and 7th GCCP had been dropped in an attempt to relieve the forts but were virtually wiped out in the process.

At least partially in response to this defeat, Marshal de Lattre de Tassigny became the new Commander in Chief in Indo-China on 17 December 1950. In an effort to raise morale de Lattre immediately used his expanded powers to instill discipline among the troops and to recruit French civilians in Indo-China to take over some of the static defensive positions which had sapped mobility by tying down regulars to garrison duties.

Operating out of two main naval bases at Cam Ranh Bay and Cape St. Jacques as well as numerous smaller bases in the delta regions or elsewhere on inland waterways, French naval strength reached 12,000 of which 10,000 were assigned to riverine, amphibious, or logistic duties. The six dinassauts were assigned as follows: four in Cochin China/Cambodian deltas and two in Tonkin.

Militarily, French fortunes took an upturn in early 1951 under de Lattre. In an attempt to test the new French commander, General Giap attacked at Vinh Yen. Two French mobile groups (roughly equivalent to U.S. regimental combat teams) defended the approaches. Group 1 was composed primarily of Goums from North Africa, while Group 3 contained Muong tribesmen and Senegalese as part of its component. Giap's forces struck on 13 January and had early successes, but on the 14th de Lattre flew into Vinh Yen to take personal command. The North African mobile group – Group 1 – fought exceptionally well, but by the 16th, the Viet Minh were launching human wave attacks and were driving the defenders back.

De Lattre called in massive air support which dropped napalm on the attacking Communists. The newly formed Mobile Group 2 – comprised of two Moroccan and one para battalion – was thrown into the battle on 17 January and along with the massive air support helped defeat Giap's forces.

During March men of the RICM (Moroccan Colonial Infantry Regiment) and of the 6th BCCP saw heavy fighting near Mao Khe. The Viet Minh also launched another heavy attack on 29 May against Ninh Binh in an attempt to breach the Red River line. Lt Bernard de Lattre, the C. in C.'s son, died in this battle. Eighty Marine Commandos of the 3rd Dinassaut also fought heroically in the defense of Ninh Binh, losing sixty-one of their number in the process. Three mobile groups, the 7th BCCP, and artillery and armored units were rapidly rushed in to reinforce the French positions by 1 June, and by 18 June the attack had been repulsed.

Though not decisive, Vinh Yen, Mao Khe, and Ninh Binh had been French victories. As a result of these repulses in the first half of 1951, the Viet Minh attempted to penetrate the strategic T'ai Mountain country. By 5 October the Viet Minh had been forced to retreat from this objective, however. Hoping to gain an advantage and pull the Viet Minh away into a classic 'set piece' battle, de Lattre struck towards the important Communist supply center at Hoa Binh.

On 14 November 2000 paras from the 1st, 2nd, and 7th BPC (as of de Lattre's March, 1951, order, GCCP was re-designated BPC [Bataillon de Parachutistes Coloniaux]) jumped on Hoa Binh and occupied the city. Fifteen infantry

battalions, seven artillery battalions, two armored groups, and two dinassauts followed up the airborne assault on land and river. Giap refused combat, however, instead deciding to encircle the French force at Hoa Binh. Heavy fighting continued along the Black River line during December with the Viet Minh slowly tightening a noose around the French positions at Hoa Binh. In December the French committed Mobile Groups 1, 4, and 7 and the 1st Airborne Group as well as supporting armored units, but the Communists faded away, only to return in early January, 1952. The dinassauts had fought heroically during December, keeping the Black

This paratrooper at Dien Bien Phu illustrates uniform items typical of the 'paras' in the later stages of the Indochina conflict. His hat is the large brimmed 'fatigue' or 'utility' camouflage hat favored by many paras. He wears the camo jump smock and carries the folding stock U.S. M1A1 .30 carbine.

River open as a means of supply and communication for Hoa Binh. During 1951 the French had managed to repulse Giap's attempts to rest control of the Red River Delta, but for most of the year they had been on the defensive rather than the offensive. One important step taken in 1951 was the formation of the GCMA (Groupement de Commandos Mixtes Aéroportés). The GCMA functioned much as the U.S. Special Forces would later, forming local guerrilla groups to fight against the Communists.

1952 began with the situation at Hoa Binh deteriorating rapidly. De Lattre had returned to France to die of cancer, and General Raoul Salan had taken his place. On 12 January 1952 the Communists managed to close the Black River to French traffic leaving Road 6 the only possible supply route to Hoa Binh. In an attempt to cut the road on 8 January the Viet Minh attacked positions of the 2nd Battalion of the Foreign Legion's 13th Demi-Brigade at Xom Pheo. Finally, after a bayonet charge in classic Legion fashion, the attack was repulsed, but only after heavy losses on both sides.

As a result of other attacks the Viet Minh also managed to cut Road 6. Finally, after taking eleven days to fight their way 25 miles between the Day River and Hoa Binh, Colonel Gilles' task force managed to break through to Hoa Binh. Salan decided in an operation code-named 'Amaranth' to evacuate Hoa Binh. With heavy air and artillery support, the evacuation was successfully carried out between 22 and 24 February.

For the next six months fighting was sporadic, with the French remaining primarily in their strong points. Small patrols were mounted around French positions and between the tiny 'mile forts', but at night the French withdrew into their fortifications. Mobile groups led by such men as Vanuxem, de Castries, Gilles, and Langlais ventured forth to keep supply lines open, but the area of French control was shrinking and French initiative was being sapped. One notable exception was the amphibious operation ('Sauterelle') carried out in August on the coast above the Perfume River. This operation and its follow-up resulted in more than 3000 Viet Minh killed or captured. In October Giap launched an attack on the strategic Nghia Lo ridge which he captured. After Nghia Lo fell it seemed impossible for the other forts in the T'ai Hills to hold.

On 16 October the 6th BCP led by Major Marcel Bigeard jumped to reinforce the French post at Tu Le and to hold while men of the 1st

T'ai Mountain Battalion, 17th Moroccan Tabor, and 3rd Battalion, 1st Moroccan Rifles pulled back. The 6th BCP was attacked on 20 October and staged a fighting retreat over 40 miles to the Black River, finally arriving on 22 October after having lost three-fifths of the battalion.

By November the occupation of the T'ai hills by the Viet Minh was virtually complete (though some GCMA units continued to operate in Communist controlled territory).

The French had set up a defensive line of sorts along the Black River, but Salan knew it would not hold against a determined Communist assault. To force Giap to withdraw his units along the Black River, Salan decided to strike with the largest French operation of the war – 'Operation Lorraine'.

30,000 French troops were gathered for 'Lorraine'. Included were four mobile groups, an airborne group, a dinassaut group, and supporting armor, artillery, and engineers. This operation was intended to progress in four stages. In the first, beginning on 29 October, a bridgehead across the Red River towards Phu Tho would be established. In the second, this bridgehead would be enlarged, and a task force driving north along Road 2 was to link up with the bridgehead. These two groups would then continue north towards Phu Doan where Airborne Group 1 (composed of the 1st and 2nd BEP and the 3rd BPC) would drop to meet the advancing task

---

FRANCE

GCMA The Groupement de Commandos Mixtes Aéroportés functioned during the Indo-China War much as the U.S. Special Forces did during the Vietnam War, working with indigenous hill people such as the T'ais to form irregular forces. This member of the GCMA, probably an NCO, wears a camo jacket of the type favored by some of the commando units and khaki drill shorts. His footgear is the French patrol boot, similar to the U.S. sneaker. He wears a khaki drill bush hat with his GCMA pocket crest affixed, a practice which, though non-regulation, was often practised. His weapon is the MAT49 SMG. **Lieutenant, 13ème DBLE** This lieutenant wears the green fatigue uniform with his 13th DBLE pocket crest on a fob over his right breast. Lieutenants rank insignia is worn on his shoulder slide. His boots are brown ankle length ones, possibly of French – but also possibly of U.S. – origin. On his képi he wears the silver grenade cap badge of the 13th DBLE. **Paratrooper, 1er BEP** This Legion para wears the U.S. spotted camo jacket used during World War II in the Pacific theater. Green French fatigue trousers are worn with brown para boots. His helmet is the U.S. M1 paratroopers helmet with net cover. His webbed gear is also of U.S. origin as is his M1A1 carbine with folding stock extended.

FRANCE

GCMA

Paratrooper, 1er BEP

Lieutenant, 13ème DBLE

French parachutist, just landed at Dien Bien Phu, offers a good view of the jump smock with the skirt snapped around the legs for the jump.

A good view of the tanker's helmet. The anchor badge probably indicates he is assigned to a colonial unit. The men in the background wear jungle hats.

force. A dinassaut would move up the Red River to prevent the enemy escaping by water. In the third stage, the now combined French force would destroy enemy supply depots in the Phu Doan area, thus – it was assumed – drawing the Communist troops to defend their supply centers. The fourth stage would consist of exploitation of successes and driving further into Communist territory.

By 4 November three bridgeheads had been secured across the Red River and Mobile Groups 1 and 4 had begun their drive towards Road 2. Beginning on 9 November, these two groups and the remainder of the task force began advancing along Road 2 with tanks and armored cars in the lead. The 3rd Dinassaut was moving up river towards the area where the airborne troops would be dropped. By 1500 hours on 9 November over 2350 paras had landed near Phu Doan and the dinassaut had arrived at the rendezvous. Mobile Groups 1 and 4 had also arrived and fanned out around the village which – as expected – proved to be a Viet Minh supply depot. With Phu Doan captured after only light resistance, the French decided to push further north.

By 14 November tanks and supporting infantry had reached Phu Yen Binh, 40 miles northwest of Phu Doan. On that date, however, because the operation had failed in its main intent of drawing Viet Minh forces into combat and because of the difficulty in keeping these extended forces supplied, withdrawal began.

By 17 November all elements had been pulled back to Phu Doan and the withdrawal south along Road 2 had commenced. In the Chan Muong Valley, however, the withdrawing column ran into a well-placed ambush. Men of the BMI (Bataillon de Marche Indochinois) – a mixed Cambodian, Vietnamese, and French unit; 2nd Battalion, 2nd REI; and 4th Battalion, 7th Algerian Rifles were caught in the middle of an ambush. Despite heavy casualties these units managed to counterattack and clear the valley, but the French had lost a dozen vehicles, 56 dead, 125 wounded, and 133 missing. By 1 December, the French had completely withdrawn all elements of the 'Lorraine' task force across the Red River. 'Lorraine' was not only a failure but one in which the French suffered heavy casualties.

As 1952 ended there were 175,000 regular troops committed to the war in Indo-China – 54,000 of them French, 30,000 North Africans, 18,000 Africans, 20,000 Legionnaires, and 53,000 Indo-Chinese. There were also 5000 members of the French Navy and 10,000 members of the Air Force. The Vietnamese National Army consisted of 50,000 men, the Laotian Army of 15,000 men, and the Cambodian Army of 10,000 men. Despite these numbers the Viet Minh, however, continued to gain ground.

French resources became stretched even more in April, 1953, as the Viet Minh expanded their theater of operations by moving into northern Laos. France did not have the reserves available to reinforce troops in Laos so French outposts were given orders to hold as long as they could while some sort of defensive line was established.

In July, 1953, 'Operation Camargue' was launched to clean the Communists from along the portion of Road 1 known as the 'Street Without Joy'. A combined airborne, amphibious, and ground operation was mounted under the command of General Leblanc.

This operation effectively encircled the Viet Minh 95th Regiment east of Road 1. The first real resistance came at the village of Dong Que when the 6th Moroccan Spahis and 1st Battalion, Moroccan Rifles ran into an ambush. Virtually a whole Viet Minh company was eliminated in the fire fight but the delay allowed the remainder of the regiment to retreat towards the southern portion of the pocket.

To help block the retreat, the 2nd Battalion, 1st RCP was dropped near the village of Dai Loc at 1045 and began driving towards the mouth of the Van Trinh Canal to complete the encirclement of the remainder of the Viet Minh regiment. Beginning at 1650 men from the 3rd BPVN (Bataillon de Parachutistes Vietnamiens) were dropped near Lang Bao despite 30 mph (48 kmph) gusts which made airborne operations very hazardous, especially for the light Vietnamese paras. Despite injuries and loss of equipment, however, the men of the 3rd BPVN managed to help close the southern escape routes. The pocket was not as tightly sealed as the French had hoped, though, and during the night of 28/29 July most of the remaining Communist troops managed to slip through gaps in the French encirclement. On 4 August 'Camargue' officially ended, a limited success in that Road 1 was re-opened and a Viet Minh company had been destroyed, but the major enemy force had slipped away because the French forces were spread too thin to truly seal the area.

On 20 November 1953 an airborne assault was undertaken to recapture the airstrip at Dien Bien Phu in order to block the Viet Minh invasion route into Laos. Airborne Battle Group I, composed of the 1st BPC, 6th BPC, and the 2nd Battalion, 1st RCP, made the initial jump into DZs 'Natasha' and 'Simone' against relatively light opposition. Airborne Battle Group II, comprised of the 1st BEP, 5th BPVN, and 8th BP Choc, reinforced Group I the next day.

In all 4525 paras came in on D-Day. During the next few days the air strip was refurbished and defensive positions were built. At the end of November, however, some of the paras began to pull out to be replaced by 'leg' infantry.

As Giap moved his units towards Dien Bien Phu in late November, the French began turning it into a fortress (at least in name if not in fact) in preparation for the 'set piece' battle they had been hoping for. By the end of 1953 nearly 5000 French troops were at Dien Bien Phu and the stage was set for the decisive battle of the war.

One other point of note occurred during November, 1953. Groupement Mobile 100 was activated in Indo-China. One of the principal components of this unit was the French Bataillon de Corée (Korea Battalion) comprised of men who had fought with the French forces in Korea.

At the end of 1953 the GCMA was renamed the GMI (Groupement Mixtes d'Intervention). Under its leader Major Roger Trinquier, the GMI would control 15,000 irregulars by 1954.

By January, 1954, as the Viet Minh built up forces around Dien Bien Phu, General Navarre, who had replaced Salan as commander in May, 1953, made the decision to pour men and equipment into Dien Bien Phu in an attempt to decisively defeat the Viet Minh. Infantry, armor, and artillery were sent to Dien Bien Phu in December, 1953, and January, 1954. Included in the artillery units arriving in December were the III/10th RAC (3rd Artillery Group, 10th Colonial Artillery Regiment), II/4th RAC, and 1st Foreign Legion Airborne Heavy Mortar Company. By early 1954 many of the parachute units had been pulled out to act as a theater reserve. The II/1st RCP, 1st BPC, and 5th BPVN had all left Dien Bien Phu, and in their place were more heavily armed infantry units such as the 13th DBLE, 3rd and 7th RTA (Algerian Rifles), 4th RTM (Moroccans), 2nd REI, and 2nd and 3rd BT (T'ai), 3rd REI, and 1st RTA. Paras from the 1st BEP and 8th BPC remained as the part of the garrison of Dien Bien Phu normally charged with aggressive patrolling. Tanks were supplied by the 1st RCC. Neither airlift nor materials were available, however, to prepare fortifications which could withstand an artillery barrage. Nevertheless, beginning on 31 January, 1954, Dien Bien Phu came under Communist artillery fire, and French patrols during February constantly encountered Viet Minh forces surrounding the area.

The real assault on Dien Bien Phu began on 12 March with attacks on 'Gabrielle', one of the outlying French strongpoints to the north of the main positions. By 13 March the other northern strongpoints – 'Anne-Marie' and 'Beatrice' had fallen despite a heroic defense by men of the 13th DBLE. On 15 March the men of the 7th Algerian Rifles defending 'Gabrielle' also had to be evacuated. By 18 March 'Anne-Marie' had also fallen, and the Communists now had positions which allowed their artillery to interdict Dien Bien Phu's airstrip.

Beginning on 30 March the Viet Minh attacked other outposts. 'Dominique' was attacked first with 'Eliane' and 'Huguette' being attacked soon after. The Viet Minh scored initial successes, but counterattacks by men of the 1st BEP, 8th BPC, 6th BPC, and 5th BPVN (the latter of which had parachuted in early in March as reinforcements) had recaptured 'Dominique' and parts of 'Eliane' by 6 April. Reinforcements from the II/1st RCP had also jumped in on 3/4 April. Some non-parachute qualified replacements with needed skills jumped into Dien Bien Phu at this time as well.

Although there was a lull in the fighting after the counterattacks of 2/5 April, Communist trenches grew closer and closer to the French positions, and French supplies of ammunition continued to shrink. France's limited air transport capacity was already overtaxed and need for aerial resupply at Dien Bien Phu grew every day. The 1800 defenders of 'Isabelle', the position to the south of the main defenses, were virtually sealed off by 7 April as three battalions of the 304th Viet Minh Division had dug trenches all around them. 'Isabelle's' commander LTC (later Col.) André Lalande of the Foreign Legion was one of the most competent officers at Dien Bien Phu and through outstanding leadership held 'Isabelle' despite constant artillery barrages.

By early April some North Africans and many of the T'ais had also begun to desert, thus increasing the burden on the other defenders of Dien Bien Phu.

Beginning on the night of 9 April, reinforcements from the 2nd BEP parachuted into Dien Bien Phu. The tough Legion paras were needed to help the legendary Marcel Bigeard and his 6th BPC in hand-to-hand fighting around 'Eliane 1'. In the battle for 'Eliane 1', eventually the 1st BEP, II/1st RCP, 5th BPVN, 6th BPC, and 2nd BEP all took part. The successes of the paratroops soon put the battle in the hands of what Bernard Falls calls 'the paratroop mafia.' By 1 April LTC Langlais, in charge of the airborne forces at Dien Bien Phu, had taken over much of the command responsibility from de Castries.

Despite the successes around 'Eliane' the Communist artillery pounding continued during the first two weeks in April. Beginning on 14 April, rations were cut back because of a food shortage, and many critical medical supplies were also short. 'Huguette', the central outpost to the northwest of the main defenses, was now under heavy attack, and supply drops became even more difficult because of ever increasing Communist AA fire. Throughout the second half of April, the Communists were wearing away the defenses of 'Huguette'. During the last week in April, the monsoon began, completely water-logging many of the French positions and making conditions even more difficult.

On 14 April Navarre ordered 'Operation Condor' (the relief of Dien Bien Phu from Laos) implemented. Plans were also made to order 'Operation Albatross' – the breakout of the Dien Bien Phu garrison towards Laos.

Among forces earmarked for 'Condor' were the 4th and 5th BCL (Bataillon Chasseurs Laotiens), 1st BPL, and II/2nd REI. As this relief force moved towards Dien Bien Phu they were to be supported by GMI units which had infiltrated

---

FRANCE

Seaman French naval uniforms during the Indo-China War differed little from the tropical uniform worn by the French Navy during World War II. This sailor wears white blouse, trousers and sailors hat, all virtually identical to the World War II pattern. **Lieutenant Colonel Pierre Langlais** Langlais, who led the 'paratroop mafia' at Dien Bien Phu, wears camo paras trousers but is not wearing his smock, wearing, instead, the khaki shirt often worn beneath the para smock. French paras normally preferred the metal parachutists wings, but Langlais was often photographed wearing the cloth wings on his right breast when wearing the khaki shirt. Lieutenant colonels rank is worn on his shoulder slides. He wears Colonel Paratroops beret and paratroopers jump boots. **Aéronavale Pilot** This pilot wears the voluminous flying overall favored by many pilots in Indo-China. His peaked service hat bears the non-general officers hat badge, and three stripes to designate his rank – captain. He wears a life vest and white flying gloves and carries his hardened leather flying helmet.

FRANCE

Seaman

Aéronavale Pilot

Lieutenant Colonel
Pierre Langlais

In the background are men of the Foreign Legion wearing the summer weight khaki shirt and trousers and blue sash. Captain Valerie André (saluting) wears her white medical uniform (she was an M.D.). On her right breast she wears both parachutists brevet and helicopter pilots wings. She jumped to give medical aid and also rescued 67 men from behind enemy lines in her helicopter.

into the area. By 23 April lead elements of the 'Condor' force were within 19 miles (50 km.) of 'Isabelle,' but the GAP (airborne group formed of the 1st and 3rd BPVN) which had been promised to drop as reinforcements could not be transported to the drop zone near Nga Na Song. In effect, this forced Mobile Group North – the relief column – to establish defensive positions on the north shore of the Nam Ou and halt their advance.

By 2 May strongpoints had begun to fall both to the northeast and northwest of Dien Bien Phu. A portion of the 1st BCP was dropped on 2 May

in an attempt to reinforce the garrison, but it seemed obvious that the end was near. By 3 May some consideration was given to dropping the newly arrived 7th BPC and 3rd BEP, but they were held in reserve, possibly for use as part of 'Condor' should it get rolling again.

Each day during the first week in May the perimeter of Dien Bien Phu shrank making it harder for the aircraft supplying the garrison to drop their supplies inside the defenses of Dien Bien Phu.

On the night of 6 May, the final Communist assault began. Under heavy artillery fire and

Algerian troops in review order. Their uniform is most distinctive: their turbans bear a gold crescent badge and a sash is worn with it. Both khaki/light brown and OD uniforms were worn by the Algerians. Turbans were usually white. Diamond shaped unit insignia is worn on the left sleeve. The men in the foreground carry MSA36s.

human wave attacks, the remaining strongpoints began to fall. On the morning of 7 May units were hastily assembled to attempt a breakout, but it was decided that the defenders were too worn down to succeed, and between 1700 and 1730 hours the main portion of Dien Bien Phu fell. 'Isabelle' held out longer, and some members of its garrison unsuccessfully tried to break out that night. By the morning of 8 May 'Isabelle' had also ceased fighting.

During the battle of Dien Bien Phu, French losses amounted to 2240 killed and 6462 wounded. In addition, more than 7000 (some sources give figures as high as 11,000) were taken prisoner after the fall of Dien Bien Phu. Some 78 men did manage to escape from Dien Bien Phu either as the battle ended or within a few days after its fall.

Colonel of the French Marine Commandos wearing dark blue/black beret, Naval Commando shoulder insignia and camouflage smock, with parachutist's brevet on his right breast. Beret badge would probably be the shield shaped badge of the Marine Commandos. His decorations include the Légion d'Honneur, the Croix de Guerre, and Croix de Guerre-T.O.E.

Upon learning of the fall of Dien bien Phu, the 'Condor' force retreated as hastily as possible. Many of them were so bitter over Hanoi's 'sellout' that they deserted after reaching safety. Other fighting continued during May, June, and July despite the crushing defeat at Dien Bien Phu. Groups 11 and 100, for example, saw especially heavy action, Group 100 being decimated by the time of the cease-fire which finally went into effect on 1 August.

France's bargaining position at Geneva had been severely undermined after the fall of Dien Bien Phu, and the partition of Vietnam into North and South on 21 July 1954 was one which was favorable to the Communists. By September, 1954, the U.S.A. had already stepped into the vacuum which would be left by the departing French and formed SEATO (Southeast Asia Treaty Organization), setting the stage for U.S. involvement in the second Indo-China War.

During October French troops were pulled out of Tonkin – now North Vietnam. The individual French soldier had fought courageously, but the lack of equipment, air support, and manpower, combined with indecisive leadership in the higher levels of command and the lack of support for the war at home had doomed the French to defeat. In all, 75,867 French Union troops were killed or missing in action and 65,125 were wounded during the Indo-China War. About 20,000 of those who died in Indo-China were from metropolitan France, and a large percentage of these were officers. This was, of course, a heavy drain on the future leadership of the French Army. Saint-Cyr graduates among the dead numbered 800 officers. In addition the national armies of the Indo-China states fighting with the French suffered 31,716 casualties.

Many Frenchmen felt that the U.S.A. had sold them out by not giving more support to the war in Indo-China. This would be balanced by the American feeling during the Vietnam War that

France, General Insignia
Front row, left to right: 1er Bataillon de Parachutistes Laotiens crest; 1er Bataillon de Parachutistes Vietnamiens crest; 3e Bataillon de Parachutistes Vietnamiens crest. *Second row:* 7e Bataillon Colonial de Commandos Parachutistes crest; 35e Regiment D'Artillerie Legére Parachutiste crest; 13eme Demi-Brigade de Legion Etrangérè crest. *Third row:* 5eme Regiment Etranger D'Infanterie crest; 1er Regiment Etranger de Cavalerie crest; 2eme Bataillon Etranger de Parachutistes crest. *Fourth row:* Brevet Militaire de Parachutiste (left and center); Commandos Marine beret badge.

Marcel Bigeard, C.O. of the 6th Colonial Paratroops, confers with other para officers. Note the baggy camo trousers worn by the paras.

French Naval Commando wearing naval style denim shirt and trousers. His hat is not a typical jungle hat and may be a fatigue hat worn by naval personnel. His weapon is the semi-automatic MAS49 in 7.5 mm, which has an integral grenade launcher; a grenade is attached ready for firing. Note the vest arrangement for extra rifle grenades.

the French gave too much support to the Communists. Both Indo-China wars led to recriminations, and both had far-reaching effects on the nations involved. Except for a few advisory missions, French troops had almost all left Indo-China by 1956, many for a new war in Algeria. Even the Algerian war had some of its roots in the defeat in Indo-China. Many FLN leaders, in fact, were Algerians who had been captured at Dien Bien Phu and brainwashed by the Communists. The fact that a liberation front had defeated the French in Indo-China was not lost on the FLN either. At least some of the disillusionment felt by the French Army in Algeria could also be traced to the recent experience in Indo-China as well. What is most unfortunate, perhaps, about the French experience in Indo-China is that the U.S.A. learned very little from it.

Uniforms and Equipment

France entered the Indo-China War with a mixture of U.S., British, and French uniforms and equipment and for the first few years of the war some odd combinations might be encountered. By 1950 uniforms had begun to take on a more typical French appearance, though U.S. gear and arms were still quite likely to be encountered.

Headgear was probably the most markedly French uniform component. Standard with most uniforms was the traditional képi. Both khaki and colored képis were worn, the képi color being determined by the arm of service. The infantry képi, for example, was dark blue with a red top. Artillery, signals, and engineers all wore a black képi, while the Foreign Legion wore the dark blue with red of the infantry. Of course, the famous white képi cover (képi blanc) of the Legion was also worn for dress occasions. Typically, the Légionnaires wore the képi in combat far more often than other units. Even at Dien Bien Phu, men of the 13th DBLE might be seen wearing their képis.

Side or field caps in the same color combinations were also worn by Army personnel. Members of the Air Force wore an all blue sidecap, while some French Union troops wore their own distinctive field caps. The Spahis, for example, wore red ones. Both officers and NCOs rank insignia was worn on the field cap.

A khaki beret was sometimes worn by French troops and was also adopted by the indigenous

Although this mortarman's unit is not identified he is probably with the 1st BEP who favored the World War II Pacific Theater camouflage shirt he is wearing. His hat is the floppy French jungle hat; his trousers are green.

Indo-Chinese armies. Special berets were worn by French elite units. Until March, 1951, some paras wore blue berets, but in that month General de Lattre ordered standardization on a red Basque beret with the winged-arm-holding-a-sword beret badge still worn by Foreign Legion paras. These Legionnaires had been wearing green berets, but de Lattre ordered them to wear the white képi. At various times, Marine Commandos wore either dark blue-black or green berets.

Floppy French jungle hats similar to those later associated with the Viet Cong and camouflage boonie hats were also widely worn. A camo 'fatigue' hat was frequently worn by the paras in lieu of the beret.

The most commonly encountered steel helmet was the U.S. M1 or M1 paratrooper's helmet with net cover and its distinctive para's chin strap. Other headgear worn at least occasionally by French or French Union troops included camouflage berets, tankers helmets, and various types of tribal headgear worn by the Berbers or Senegalese. Tankers it should be noted were usually assigned to cavalry units in Vietnam and thus would have worn the light blue képi. Indo-Chinese paras sometimes jumped in a very noticeable flat padded helmet, though this was used more often for training jumps than combat jumps.

Uniforms were also quite varied within the French Union forces and even within individual units. Widely worn – especially by officers – was the khaki bush shirt with epaulets and khaki trousers or shorts. A leather fob worn on the right pocket of this or other uniforms often bore the unit crest. American style green fatigues were also widely issued during the latter years of the war. Shoulder sleeve insignia were sometimes worn on the 'greenies'. Indo-Chinese units were often issued green, brown, khaki, or even black cloth utilities, in some cases with shorts not trousers.

Paras wore a distinctive camouflage smock and camouflage trousers. The men assigned to the GCMA sometimes wore British SAS camo smocks. Various British, U.S.M.C., or other camouflage uniforms were also worn. Legion paras, especially, were issued U.S.M.C. World War II spotted camo suits. Pilots normally wore the khaki bush shirt and trousers or the green U.S. style fatigues. Members of dinassauts also wore these uniforms, though shorts were favored. Some members of riverine forces – especially the Marine Commandos – wore camouflage uniforms, though they wore camouflage shirts normally rather than para smocks. The most common camouflage pattern was what is usually known as 'lizard' pattern. Even the uniforms issued with full length trousers were 'field expediently' altered to shorts either by cutting off the pant legs or by rolling them up.

As with other uniform items the earliest French units in Indo-China were normally equipped with American or British combat

These Cambodian machine-gunners wear the jungle hat worn almost universally by French Union forces. Note also the light rucksack and the Bren gun. Cambodians looked very different from the Vietnamese, being much darker and having different features. There was much distrust of American blacks by the Vietnamese because the Viets thought the blacks resembled Cambodians who were their traditional enemies.

boots. Throughout the war there remained, however, a diversity of issue footwear. Most common was probably the ankle high three-quarter hob-nailed boot. Also widely worn was the canvas and rubber jungle boot which was, in effect, a sneaker. Though comfortable, this boot and the French technique of searching for Viet Minh arms caches by walking barefoot through rice paddies made for a lot of punji spike wounds. Although the paras often wore either of these other types of boots, they were normally issued a high top, cleated jump boot which gave more ankle and leg support while jumping. Sandals were worn by some Indo-Chinese troops, and in some instances French troops also adopted sandals for local wear.

Although webbed or leather gear of both British and French pattern was sometimes issued, the closest to standard was the British 1937 pattern web equipment worn in the early post-war years by units which had served with British equipped Free French forces or the

Members of the Demi-Brigade de Parachutistes SAS march through Hanoi in 1948, wearing camouflage smocks with green trousers bloused into the jump boots. The beret badge is Malcros 55, later adapted by the 1er RPIMa.

standard U.S. webbed gear issued to veterans of American equipped Free French units. Some pieces of French M1935 equipment such as the leather belt and ammo pouches were still issued, especially to some of the colonial troops. U.S. World War II webbed gear remained, however, the most commonly issued. As new French arms such as the MAT 49 were introduced French magazine pouches, etc. were also introduced for them. Other than some paras or the GCMA and occasional Legion units, French troops rarely operated on deep penetration missions, hence packs were not frequently worn. When packs were used either American or British World War II types were issued or a smaller rucksack was used. At least a few British Bergen rucksacks were in use with the GCMA.

Depending upon the uniform and headgear, various types of insignia were worn. Battalion or regimental crests were often worn on a fob attached to the right pocket. Occasionally, these crests might also be pinned directly to the pocket or to the headgear. Paras wore the winged-hand-clutching-a-sword badge on their berets. Diamond-shaped shoulder sleeve insignia in different colors to designate branch and bearing numerical unit designations were also worn. On the right breast the parachutist's brevet, normally in metal but sometimes in cloth, was worn when airborne qualified. On the camouflage smock or shirt, however, the para brevet was often deleted. Some paras wore jump wings on the khaki shirt beneath the camo smocks.

Officers rank was worn on epaulets and also on the képi or field cap. The background color on these epaulets indicated branch. At Dien Bien Phu, for example, when Col. de Castries was promoted to brigadier and Lt Col. Langlais was promoted to colonel, de Castries passed his rank insignia on to Langlais who had to color de Castries' red cavalryman's background black with india ink since he was a para.

In the French Army a Général d'Armée (general) wore five stars, a Général de Corps d'Armée (lieutenant general) wore four stars, a Général de Division (major general) wore three stars, and a Général de Brigade (brigadier) wore two stars. A colonel wore five gold bars, a lieutenant colonel three gold bars alternating with two silver bars, a commandant (major) four gold bars, a capitaine (captain) three gold bars, a lieutenant two gold bars, and a sous-lieutenant (second lieutenant) one gold bar. An aspirant (officer cadet) wore a red curl, an adjudant-chef (warrant officer 1st class) a narrow red stripe centered in a broad yellow stripe, and an adjutant (warrant officer 2nd class) a narrow red stripe centered in a broad white stripe.

NCOs chevrons were worn point up on the sleeve with the diamond-shaped unit patch in the notch of the chevrons. A sergent-major (master sergeant) wore four gold chevrons, a sergent-chef (sergeant 1st class) three gold chevrons, a sergent (sergeant) one gold and one red chevron, a caporal-chef (corporal 1st class) one gold and two red chevrons, a caporal (corporal) two red chevrons, and a soldat de première classe (PFC) one red chevron.

Air Force officers and NCOs ranks were the same as the Army's except that there was an additional sergeant's rank – sergent de carrière (professional sergeant) – between sergent-chef and sergent. The sergent de carrière wore two gold chevrons and the sergent one gold chevron. Air Force NCOs wore their rank insignia on epaulets instead of on their sleeves. Pilots wore their wings on their right breasts.

Naval insignia for officers was roughly similar to Army insignia except that the bars were worn on the sleeve and edge of the shoulder rather than epaulets. Naval NCOs rank was designated by a series of half chevrons. Three gold half chevrons designated a maître (chief petty officer), two gold half chevrons a second maître, classe 1 (petty officer 1st class), and one gold half chevron a second maître (petty officer 2nd class). Different classes of seamen were designated by one, two, or three red half chevrons.

Once again the assortment of weapons in use in Indo-China was indicative of the fact that the early post-war French Army was heavily dependent upon the U.S.A. and Great Britain for arms. Handguns in use by officers or others issued sidearms included the U.S. Colt 1911 auto, the French M1935 auto, and – in the latter part of the war – the French M1950 auto. One of the most commonly issued weapons in Indo-China was the American M1 Carbine. The selective fire M2 and the folding stock M1A1 paratrooper carbine also saw wide use among the paras. British SMLE bolt action rifles, American M1 Garands, French MAS 36 bolt action rifles and French MAS 36CR39 folding stock paratrooper carbines were also widely used. Although in the early years of the war British Sten guns and U.S. M3 'Grease-guns' and M1A1 Thompsons were the primary SMGs, by the 1950s the French MAT 49 had become widely standardized.

2 The Special Forces and the CIDG Program

Among the first American troops to arrive in the Republic of Vietnam and among the last to leave were the Special Forces. As early as 1957 members of the Special Forces were acting as advisors to the Vietnamese Rangers and airborne units. The year 1960 also saw the arrival in Laos of more than a hundred Green Berets under the command of 'Bull' Simons to train Muong tribesmen to fight against the Communists.

Training local irregulars such as the Muongs or acting as advisors to special units such as the Republic of Vietnam Army (ARVN) Rangers or paratroopers were specialties of the Green Berets who had been formed in 1952 to carry out missions behind enemy lines. They traced their military lineage from such illustrious predecessors as the OSS, 1st Special Service Force, and Rangers of World War II. Although the Special Forces were trained primarily to form local guerrilla groups behind enemy lines, they found themselves becoming guerrilla hunters rather than guerrillas in Vietnam. As it worked out they performed their new mission exceptionally well and even turned the tables on the Viet Cong (VC) irregulars by leading Vietnamese irregulars deep into VC territory.

The Special Forces really began to make their presence felt – both quantitatively and qualitatively – with the beginnings of the Civilian Irregular Defense Group (CIDG) program in 1961. The aim of the CIDG program was to train members of local minority groups such as the Montagnards to protect themselves and their local areas from the VC. This would serve the dual purpose of taking some of the fighting burden off of regular ARVN units and of eliminating some of the fear of the VC by equipping minorities – especially in the strategic Central Highlands – to defend themselves. The first priority was training a local hamlet militia, and once this was accomplished in an area, mobile units capable of taking limited offensive action or serving as a mobile reserve would be formed.

The largest minority group in Vietnam were the Montagnards, and a village of their largest tribe – the Rhade – was chosen for the pilot site in the 'Area Development Program' as the CIDG program was originally known. The village selected was Buon Enao, and seven members of the U.S. Special Forces along with some Luc Luong Duc Biet (LLDB) – the Vietnamese Special Forces – moved into the village to implement the experiment. First, an enclosure for defense of the area was built around the village, and then the training began. An unpaid hamlet militia was formed to protect the village and was armed with light small arms. A local full-time paid strike force was also recruited to act as a reserve for any village within its area of responsibility which came under attack.

The experiment proved so successful that the CIDG program moved ahead at full speed, and by August of 1962, 200 villages were under CIDG protection. There were 10,600 local militiamen and 1500 strike force members in the province, and VC activity had virtually ceased. To continue expanding the CIDG program more Special Forces troops were needed and by the end of 1962, 26, 12-man A-teams were deployed 'in country'.

The A-team was the basic operational unit of the Special Forces and was normally broken down as follows: commanding officer, normally a captain; executive officer, normally a lieutenant; operations sergeant; intelligence sergeant; heavy weapons leader; light weapons leader; medical specialist; radio operator specialist; engineer sergeant; chief of research and development operator; assistant medical specialist; and engineer assistant. Each man was cross-trained to perform at least one or more other functions so that skills were duplicated in case the team was split or suffered casualties. The medical and engineering specialists were especially important in winning the local minorities since they helped with civic action programs, one reason there were two team members with each of these skills.

The CIDG program continued its growth in 1963, and by the end of the year, there were more

U.S. Special Forces heavy weapons leader supervises Montagnard crew loading a 105 mm howitzer. Both camouflage and green utilities are worn but, except for the member of the S.F., camouflage boonie hats were 'standard'.

than 60,000 hamlet militiamen and strike force members who had been trained by the Special Forces. Even more importantly, the Special Forces had gained the respect and affection of the minorities.

The CIDG program was going so well, in fact, that in 1963 and 1964, the Special Forces began training indigenous troops for more aggressive action against the VC. Special mountain scouts, border surveillance patrols, and long range pat-rols were trained to interdict VC trail movement, and strike force members were trained as hunter groups. These early efforts were forerunners of Delta, Sigma, Omega and other MACV/SOG programs later on. Also in an attempt to secure the border against infiltration, the bulk of CIDG camps established in 1964 were along the Cambodian–Laotian border. By July, 1964, CIDG strike force troops were manning 25 border camps. The strike force company was also standardized at 150 men.

As the CIDG program continued to grow in importance, more members of the Special Forces were needed for training and advisory duties. It was also decided that the provisional units from the 1st Special Forces Group which had been operating in Vietnam on 6 month temporary duty (TDY) postings were not as effective as they might be if a Special Forces group was activated specifically for duty in Vietnam. As a result, the 5th Special Forces Group was activated for service in Vietnam. By the end of 1964, there were 45 A-teams, five B-teams, and two C-teams in country. The B-team which normally controlled four A-teams consisted of 24 men commanded by a major. Three B-teams were under the control of a C-team or Special Forces company. The C-team consisted of 19–20 men under the command of a lieutenant colonel.

In May, 1964, 'Project Leaping Lena' was implemented. Its objective was to train LLDBs and CIDGs to function as long range recon units who could penetrate behind enemy lines. 'Leaping Lena' was the beginning of Project Delta, which would eventually be organized into 12 reconnaissance teams, 12 roadrunner teams, one camp security company composed of Nungs, and an ARVN Ranger battalion as a reaction force. Among Delta's missions were location of enemy units, intelligence gathering, calling in artillery or air strikes, raids, assassinations, or any other harassment of the enemy in his 'safe' areas. Roadrunner teams wore North Vietnam Army (NVA) or VC uniforms and operated along enemy trails, often mingling with infiltrating enemy units and either leading them into ambushes or attacking them from within their own ranks if an opportunity presented itself. Mobile Strike Forces – often known as MIKE Forces – were also formed in 1964 to act as an elite CIDG reserve unit which was directly under Special Forces control.

To eliminate many of the supply problems inherent in irregular units and to bypass the corrupt Vietnamese logistical system, the Special Forces used the U.S. Army Counterinsurgency Support Office in Okinawa to set up their own supply network, many items coming from CIA sources, while others were acquired locally or wherever possible. Stockpiles maintained by each B-team combined with a good air delivery system kept CIDG camps more effectively supplied than virtually any other units in Vietnam except, of course, the 'Saigon Commandos'.

1964 also saw the CIDG program suffer a real blow when Montagnards rebelled at five camps in the II Corps area. The rebellion was directed at the Vietnamese government which had long pursued a policy of treating the 'Yards' as second class citizens. Finally, the rebellion was quelled

by U.S. Special Forces officers – none of whom had been harmed by the Montagnards – who acted as mediators between the Montagnards and the government. Although the Special Forces managed to stop the rebellion because of the respect the Montagnards had for them, throughout the remainder of the war there was a 'Yard' underground movement against the government.

In 1965 the U.S. troop build-up in Vietnam began, and the Special Forces and the CIDG units were called upon to supply intelligence for the conventional units. CIDG patrols were used to make contact with the enemy, and then more heavily armed units of the U.S. 1st Cavalry Division (Airmobile) would be called in for the 'kill'. A classic operation of this type was 'Crazy Horse' in May, 1966.

The MIKE Forces also began to see more action after the American build-up began. Composed mostly of Nungs – ethnic Chinese with a long heritage as mercenary soldiers – the MIKE Forces were more well-trained and more heavily armed than other CIDG units. Each 500 to 600 man MIKE Force had a U.S. Special

---

U.S. ARMY SPECIAL FORCES

MIKE Force Sergeant This sergeant is assigned to one of the MIKE Forces. He wears the green beret with 5th SFG flash, tiger stripes and jungle boots. Subdued name and 'MIKE FORCE' tapes as well as subdued parachutists wings and Combat Infantryman's badges are worn on his chest. The MIKE Force insignia is also worn on his left breast pocket. His weapon is the .45 automatic pistol.

Colonel 'Bull' Simons Col. Simons, portrayed just after the Son Tay Raid which he led, was one of the most highly respected Special Forces officers. He wears his green uniform with trousers bloused into black combat boots. The Ranger tab on his right shoulder is that of his World War II unit – the 6th Ranger Bn. The bars on his right sleeve each denote six months overseas combat duty. Vietnamese parachutists wings and a Philippine Presidential Unit Citation are visible on his right breast, while U.S. master parachutists wings and Combat Infantrymans badge along with the many ribbons denoting long and courageous service adorn his left breast.

MACV/SOG Recon Team Member This figure is dressed for a covert recon mission into Laos, Cambodia, or North Vietnam. A bandanna made from an OD bandage is worn around his head. A canvas duck survival vest with sleeves and collar sewn to it is worn in lieu of a shirt. Clothing is dyed black so he can blend with the shadows better. The snap links and leg straps of his STABO rig are clearly visible. Canvas leggings are worn over the jungle boots to help keep the leeches out. Among his many weapons are a Browning Hi-Power 9 mm auto in a GI leather shoulder harness, a 'Swedish K' 9 mm SMG, a sawed off M79 grenade launcher loaded with anti-personnel rounds, a Randall fighting/survival knife and M26 grenades.

U.S. ARMY SPECIAL FORCES

MIKE Force Sergeant

Colonel 'Bull' Simons

MACV/SOG Recon Team Member

MACV/SOG team from MLT-1, c. 1970. Note the STABO rigs and OD scarfs worn on the heads. Weapons are the CAR15.

Forces A-team permanently assigned to it. Within the MIKE Forces themselves were elite combat recon platoons. The 34 men comprising each of these platoons were trained at the LLDB training center and were used for long range recon patrols, raids, ambushes, and other special missions requiring highly reliable troops. Members of these platoons were also normally airborne qualified. In July, 1966, each MIKE Force added a second recon platoon.

Also in mid-1966, the MIKE Forces were assigned stepped up patrolling and recon duties in addition to their basic mission of acting as quick reaction forces for reinforcement of CIDG camps under attack. One MIKE Force was deployed in each corps tactical zone, and one was retained at 5th Special Forces HQ at Nha Trang.

Others were deployed as follows: I Corps – Da Nang, II Corps – Pleiku, III Corps – Bien Hoa, IV Corps – Don Phuc. As the war progressed MIKE Forces were either assigned or reassigned to other camps.

MACV/SOG also increased the scope of its operations after the American build-up. Under dynamic leaders such as Col. Donald Blackburn (later Brig. Gen.) and Col. John Singlaub MACV/SOG spread its operations into Laos and Cambodia, and eventually into North Vietnam. By 1966 operations into Cambodia and Laos were undertaken as a matter of course. The rescue of downed airmen, POW rescues, intelligence gathering, deep penetration recon missions, sabotage – MACV/SOG engaged in all.

The Special Forces also established the MACV Recondo School at Nha Trang in September, 1966. Three week courses were run to train CIDG units and also U.S. Long Range Reconnaissance Patrols (LRRPs) or other allied

units. Additional combat recon platoons were also trained, and by mid-1967, 73 of them were operating out of Special Forces fighting camps throughout the country.

In the fall of 1966 two more MACV/SOG programs – Projects Omega and Sigma – were begun. Units assigned to these projects were directly under U.S. Special Forces control rather than under the LLDB with the Special Forces acting as 'advisors' as was usually the case. About 600 men were assigned to each of these projects. Eight roadrunner teams composed of four indigenous troops each and eight recon teams composed of two U.S. Special Forces and four 'indigs' each were the probe units of Omega and Sigma. Three MIKE force reaction companies were available to each project when additional firepower was needed. Roadrunners continued to operate along enemy trails wearing enemy uniforms, while recon teams gathered intelligence, sabotaged enemy installations or supply caches

'Cidgees' from a Special Forces floating camp mount the .30 caliber MGs on air boats before a Mekong Delta operation. The cidgee in the right foreground wears the older style spotted camouflage jacket with tiger stripe trousers. All figures, including the U.S. Special Forces trooper mounting the MG in the far boat, wear camouflage berets. The figure with the spotted jacket appears to have a MIKE Force beret badge.

(often by inserting ammo, grenades, mortar shells, etc. which were doctored to explode prematurely) and creating as much havoc behind enemy 'lines' as possible.

Indigenous Omega and Sigma troops attended a one week jump school and were trained in silent movement, tracking, observation, map and compass usage, signaling, infiltration and exfiltration, special weapons, treatment of wounds, and other Ranger/Recon types of skills applicable to extended operation in enemy controlled areas. Some Omega and Sigma operations lasted 30 to 60 days, resupply being via air drop. Often, to

U.S. Special Forces members instruct 'cidgees' on the M79 grenade launcher at Camp Trai Trung Sup. Note the tiger stripes, and also the green beret which is worn by the trooper in the background.

avoid giving away the SOG unit's position, supplies were dropped in dummy 500 lb (225 kg.) napalm containers seemingly as part of an attack. Any unit which ran into trouble could be quickly extracted by standby choppers.

Omega and Sigma missions normally were 'launched' from Forward Operating Bases (FOB). The three major ones were at Kontum, Da Nang, and Ban Me Thuot. These FOBs were later redesignated Command and Control Central (CCC), Command and Control North (CCN), and Command and Control South (CCS) respectively. CCC, CCN, and CCS units were organized into Spike Recon Teams composed of three Special Forces and nine indigenous personnel, Hatchet Forces composed of four Special Forces and 30 'indigs', Search-Locate-Annihilate-Mission (SLAM) Companies.

Hatchet Forces were used for large scale missions into enemy territory. From CCC, missions were launched into Laos, Cambodia, and parts of South Vietnam. From CCN, missions were launched into Laos and North Vietnam. From CCS, missions were launched into Cambodia and South Vietnam.

SPECIAL FORCES AND CIDG TRAINED IRREGULARS

Montagnard CIDG Trooper This cidgee wears the early pattern tiger-striped utilities and tiger-striped boonie hat and combat boots rather than jungle boots. He carries an M16 rifle and 1911A1 automatic pistol in a GI shoulder holster. The red scarf is for unit identification. His webbed gear is the M56 harness in 'fighting load' configuration.
Project 'Sigma' Roadrunner Since 'roadrunners' normally patrolled along the VC trail network it was standard for them to wear VC gear. As a result this figure wears black 'pajamas', VC style jungle hat, and Ho Chi Minh sandals. His webbed gear and ruck are of the type used by the VC, and his weapon is a French MAT49 SMG, also widely used by the VC. **MIKE Force Striker** This striker is probably a member of the Don Phuc MIKE Force since he is serving aboard one of the Special Forces operated airboats used for patrolling in the Mekong Delta. He wears one of the 'leopard' spotted patterns of camouflage sometimes seen on S.F. trained irregulars. Even his beret, which bears the MIKE Force insignia, is of this pattern. His weapon is the U.S. M1 .30 carbine, though M2s were also used.

SPECIAL FORCES AND CIDG TRAINED IRREGULARS

Montagnard CIDG Trooper

CIDG MIKE Force Striker

MACV/SOG Project 'Sigma' Road Runner

In 1966 and 1967 the Special Forces along with the Navy's 'Sea-Air-Land' (SEAL) and Riverine forces worked to secure the Mekong Delta. CIDG 'floating camps' were established in areas of the Delta which normally flooded. Buildings, bunkers, and helicopter pads were all constructed on floating floors which rose with the flood waters and allowed the camps to remain in operation year round, even during the monsoon. Using motorized sampans, air boats, and choppers, CIDG units struck severe blows against the VC throughout the Mekong Delta. During the monsoon in 1966–67, VC units whose movements were hampered by rain and flood were hit hard by these aquatic CIDG units. These, by the way, were not the only Special Forces waterborne operations. MACV/SOG was also involved in various types of 'psy ops'.

Regular CIDG fighting camps also began to be standardized in 1967. Using a system of defense in depth, the camps were designed to withstand massed VC attacks. Perimeters were guarded by eight 60 mm. mortars and up to 18 .30 caliber machine-guns with interlocking fields of fire. Normal complement of a fighting camp was one U.S. Special Forces A-team, four 132 man CIDG companies, two combat recon platoons, a civic action and psy ops squad, and sometimes a 105 mm. artillery section. These fighting camps were established in critical areas along the VC infiltration and supply routes and as a result sometimes came in for heavy attack.

Although trained for irregular warfare rather than fighting in built-up areas, many 'cidgees' and their Special Forces advisors saw combat in the cities during the January 1968 Tet Offensive. MIKE Force troops were involved in especially heavy fighting since many were based in key cities. Not only were Special Forces led irregulars instrumental in the defense of cities such as Nha Trang, Kontum, and Ban Me Thuot which had large contingents, but also at Qui Nhon, Pleiku, Chau Dac, Phan Thiet, and Dalat.

By 1968, 34 MIKE Force companies were deployed – five in I Corps, 12 in II Corps, seven in III Corps, and ten in IV Corps. U.S. Special Forces strength was over 2500, deployed in 80 A-teams, 16 B-teams, and five C-teams.

Because of the 'Vietnamization' policy, many CIDG camps were turned over to the Vietnamese Special Forces in 1968 and 1969. In fact, the schedule called for all CIDG operations to be under Vietnamese control by the end of 1970. This schedule was adhered to. Eighty per cent. of the 'cidgees' joined the Army of the Republic of Vietnam. Thirty-seven CIDG camps became ARVN Ranger camps, and for the first time minorities such as the Montagnards achieved full citizenship by joining the ARVN.

May, 1970, saw U.S. and Vietnamese troops moving across the border into Cambodia. Delta, Sigma, and Omega units long familiar with Communist areas from their cross-border operations provided intelligence about the locations of enemy arms and supply depots.

In November, 1970, the Special Forces mounted its most daring mission of the war. Fifty-six volunteers from the 6th and 7th Special Forces Groups led by Col. 'Bull' Simons raided Son Tay Prison in an attempt to free American prisoners of war. Unfortunately, the POWs had been moved, but the Son Tay mission was still a classic raid into enemy territory. Hundreds of Chinese or Soviet advisors quartered near Son Tay were killed, and the North Vietnamese were forced to tie down thousands of troops on garrison duties in fear of other similar raids. These troops could have, otherwise, been used against the South. The Chinese also began to doubt the ability of the North Vietnamese to defend their own territory as a result of the Son Tay raid. The raid also seemed to lend weight to former MACV/SOG CO Donald Blackburn's contention that the Special Forces should have been used much as the British Commandos were in World War II to raid dams, power plants, etc.

A little over five weeks after the Son Tay raid, the Special Forces ended their involvement with the CIDG program, and on 1 March 1971, the 5th Special Forces Group was redeployed back to Fort Bragg. Although this supposedly ended Special Forces involvement in South Vietnam, many former MACV/SOG troopers were sent back in March, 1972, to call in air strikes during the North Vietnamese invasion.

Although Special Forces operations in Vietnam have always been the most well known, there were also Special Forces camps in Cambodia, Laos, Thailand, and – according to some sources – even North Vietnam. The U.S. Army Vietnam Individual Training Group (UITG) later known as Forces Armée Nationale Khmer Training Command (FANK), for example, trained Cambodian troops between February, 1971 and November, 1972. The 46th Special Forces Company also served in Thailand from October, 1966 through April, 1974. Many MACV/SOG operations were launched from Thailand.

By the very nature of their missions, members of the Special Forces kept a low profile, yet they still received 14 Congressional Medals of Honor, six of them posthumously. Although their numbers were small when compared with the huge masses of other troops serving in Vietnam, the Special Forces influenced the war in a large way, for they managed to train their indigenous charges to travel light and fast and to hit hard – in effect, turning the VC's techniques against them.

Uniforms and Equipment

Just as their missions were often 'irregular' or 'unconventional' so frequently were the uniforms and equipment worn by members of the Special Forces. The wide diversity in uniforms, weapons, and equipment used by the Special Forces can be attributed to four main considerations. First, the Special Forces were working

81 mm mortar crew in action – note the flak jackets worn by the crew members. The figure at left has 'Spec 4' rank insignia.

with local indigenous troops and both to achieve acceptance and because of logistical considerations the same uniforms and equipment were worn. Second, the Special Forces had their own supply channels which could be counted on to obtain the best gear for the job, whether it was standard U.S. issue or not. Third, the Special Forces, especially those assigned to MACV/SOG were engaged in missions which often required special weapons or equipment. Fourth, there were local tailor shops all over Vietnam which would make up special 'cammies' or insignia, and the Special Forces were never hesitant to avail themselves of this local talent.

Most well-known item of Special Forces attire, of course, was the green beret which was worn

33

with the flash over the left eye. Enlisted personnel wore the Special Forces crossed arrows and dagger beret badge on the flash, while officers wore their rank insignia on the flash. Most commonly encountered flash was that of the 5th Special Forces Group which was black with a white border and had a wide yellow stripe (bend) containing three red stripes (bendets). These colors represented the South Vietnamese flag. In the early days, the 1st Special Forces Group's yellow flash (with black border after John F. Kennedy's death) was also worn.

Although it was distinctive the beret was not always the most practical headgear, and members of the Special Forces wore assorted headgear, including camouflage berets, ARVN Ranger berets, or, often, just an OD (olive drub) headband made from a towel or bandage. The floppy hats worn by the Vietnamese (both North and South) were also worn, especially by those such as MACV/SOG wanting to camouflage their U.S. origin. Bush or boonie hats were also widely worn.

An even wider assortment of uniforms were worn by the Special Forces and the 'cidgees'. Up until 1965 or 1966, standard green utilities were

5th SFG member instructs a MIKE Force trooper in proper parachute technique; both wear tiger stripes. Note the 5th Group beret flash with Special Forces crest. Pocket patch is of the Mobile Strike Force. Subdued (white in this case) parachutists badge and combat infantrymans badge are worn on the left breast.

U.S. Special Forces Insignia

First row, left to right: Recon Team Kentucky (SOG/CCC) patch; locally acquired SOG parachutist's wings; Recon Team Fork (SOG–CCS) patch. *Second row:* Command and Control Central (SOG) patch; locally produced 5th Special Forces Group insignia; Forward Operations Base 2 (SOG). *Third row:* Recon Team West Virginia (SOG–CCC) (Chinese characters say 'Kill VC'); Recon Team Missouri (SOG–CCN); Recon Team Moccasin (SOG–CCN). *Fourth row:* Recon Team Adder (SOG–CCN); Recon Team Colorado (SOG–CCC); Command and Control North (SOG).

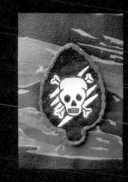

the most commonly worn, but both the Special Forces and the CIDG unit members also wore the spotted 'duck hunter' camouflage, so called because in the States it was sold for use while hunting waterfowl. Spotted World War II era camouflage uniforms were also worn. Tiger-stripe camouflage was widely worn among Special Forces, frequently purchased at the individual's expense at local military supply shops and tailored to fit. Likewise, some unique camouflage uniforms were made to order, including one the author has examined which has a leaf pattern on the front for use when standing and a brownish/ground cover pattern on the back for when lying down. 'Tiger Stripes' were identifiable by their dark blue or black stripes. In 1968, the four color (black, brown, two greens) camouflage pattern called 'leaf pattern' and often associated with Special Forces and other 'elite' units became available and received wide use among the Special Forces and their indigenous comrades. Finally, all manner of special uniforms were worn by troops assigned to MACV/SOG, including enemy uniforms and those dyed black to blend better with the shadows.

When assigned to administrative duties, members of the Special Forces might have worn the tan 'Class A's', the summer weight uniform authorized for year round wear in the Republic of Vietnam. Badges and insignia were worn with this uniform, and frequently displayed by members of the Special Forces were Vietnamese jump wings on their right breast to complement the U.S. paratrooper's wings on their left breast. Most members of Special Forces who had been assigned to 'advisory' duties in the field would also wear the combat infantryman's badge. Other decorations such as the air medal were, of course, based on the individual's combat experience. The arrowhead patch of the Special Forces was worn on the left shoulder with the AIRBORNE tab over it. For Special Forces personnel, the trousers were bloused into the combat boots.

It should be noted that the Vietnamese and U.S. paratroopers wings, combat infantryman's badge, Special Forces patch, and airborne tab were also frequently worn in subdued versions on the utilities by many members of the Special Forces. Most often these subdued para and combat infantryman's badges were in white thread but occasionally black thread was used. Subdued Special Forces patches were rare early in the war but were often seen by the late 1960s.

Originally, Special Forces wore standard black combat boots but switched almost entirely to jungle boots of fabric, leather, and rubber when they became generally available. Later pattern jungle boots incorporated an aluminum insole to protect against punji spikes. Many Special Forces also wore the olive drab tennis shoes popular with the Montagnards and known as 'Bata boots'. Enemy sandals or tennis shoes were popular with SOG team members so that they did not leave distinctive foot prints along enemy trails. Of course, finding enemy footwear in a size that would fit American personnel was difficult. An alternative which served the same purpose was to have the rubber lugs ground off of a pair of combat boots.

Generally, members of the Special Forces used the same load bearing gear as other U.S. Army units. The basic fighting load consisted of the suspenders, pistol belt with eyelets for attaching gear, universal pouches, field dressing pouch, and canteen cover with plastic canteen. Frequently, members of the Special Forces substituted indigenous rucksacks for issue ones. Members of MACV/SOG teams preferred the STABO rig which was made in Taiwan for the Central Intelligence Agency. This gear had snap links at the shoulder for chopper liftout while the hands remained free for weapons use. The nylon web harness of the STABO rig passed over the shoulders and between the legs.

A canvas Air Force survival vest was also often worn by SOG team members. Among equipment or gear carried in this vest or elsewhere by SOG team members were first aid kit, signal mirror, cut down signal panel, mini-smoke grenades, mini-grenades, gas mask, fighting/survival knife (Randalls and Gerbers were especially popular along with issue 'Jet Pilots' knives; there was also a Special Forces issue Bowie style knife), albumin blood expander, I-V tube, small rubber hose, three or more canteens, survival packets, ammunition, and URC-68 radio. A light weight rucksack was also the normal choice with SOG team members. Because they might have to depart an area suddenly, SOG members rarely took off their equipment, even sleeping in it.

The Special Forces were normally well-armed with conventional and special weapons. In the early part of the CIDG program, the 'cidgees' were usually equipped with M1 or M2 carbines and their Special Forces advisors carried the same weapons along with .45 automatic pistols. Later, as the 'indigs' were equipped with the M16 or its carbine version, the CAR15

(XM177E2), the Special Forces also started using these weapons. Short barreled 12 gauge fighting shotguns such as the Ithaca Model 37 were widely used as well.

Special Forces sergeant giving CIDG trainees hand-to-hand combat instruction, wearing his Special Forces patch and tab with green utilities.

SOG team members used the CAR15 but also carried various special weapons. The Swedish K SMG, silenced Sten gun, M16 with suppressor and/or starlight scope, and XM203 were all used by SOG team members. If on extended operations in enemy controlled territory where ammo might have to come from local sources, AK47s might also be carried. Additionally, SOG team members normally carried a silenced Hi-Standard .22 automatic pistol, a 9 mm. Browning Hi-Power, a sawed off M79 grenade launcher loaded with anti-personnel rounds, and pen-flares with special cartridges.

No other unit in Vietnam had the wealth of insignia worn by the Special Forces. Standard, of course, were the beret flash, U.S. airborne wings, and the light blue arrowhead shoulder patch with AIRBORNE tab. Special Forces advisors also wore ARVN para wings and insignia of the units they were advising. For those assigned to airborne qualified Vietnamese units, jump designator wings were also common. It was the SOG recon teams, however, who had the most colorful and interesting insignia. Unauthorized and usually produced in small quantity at local single sewing machine tailoring shops, these are among the most sought after collectables of the War.

Most frequently used theme in the SOG patches was a death's head wearing a green beret. Many CCN recon teams were assigned the names of snakes (i.e. RT Mamba, RT Adder, RT Asp) and hence bore snakes on their patches. Other recon teams bearing the names of American states sometimes had something to do with the state on the patch – Recon Team Kentucky, for example, had a horse on its patch. Daggers or swords, blood, bows and arrows (traditional Montagnard weapon), wings, and assault rifles were other frequently encountered symbols. Virtually all SOG patches were colorful – even garish – and were not displayed openly on operations. Many times, SOG patches were worn inside the beret sewn to the lining or in some other non-visible location.

3 U.S. Army

Until the spring of 1965, the U.S. Army had been functioning in an advisory role in Vietnam, but in May, 1965, the 173rd Airborne Brigade was sent to Bien Hoa. Two months later, the 1st Brigade of the 101st Airborne Division arrived, and in September, 1965, the 1st Cavalry Division (Airmobile) became the first full U.S. division in the Republic of Vietnam. It was no accident that the first three major ground units deployed were all highly mobile airborne or airmobile troops. The Viet Cong had the South Vietnamese completely on the defensive, and it was hoped crack assault troops would help turn this situation around. The 173rd Airborne's deployment

Good example of the locally produced patches which expressed the average grunt's disillusionment with the war in Vietnam: 'Sorry About That' was a favorite answer to any kind of mistake in Vietnam. The patch is a put-on of the MACV patch in the same colors but substituting the upraised finger for the upraised sword.

to Bien Hoa also reflected the MACV commander General Westmoreland's lack of confidence in the ability of South Vietnamese troops to protect U.S. aircraft.

Originally, the U.S.A. followed what was called an 'enclave strategy'. U.S. troops were committed only around key air bases, ports, etc., while fighting in the hinterlands was left to the Vietnamese. American troops did undertake limited offensive patrols, but only within 80 'klicks' (kilometers) or approximately 50 miles of their 'enclaves'. Shortly after the arrival of the airmobile units, however, the 'enclave' strategy was abandoned. Even before the end of 1965, in fact, the 1st Air Cav was involved in extensive offensive operations such as 'Silver Bayonet' in Pleiku Province against NVA regulars. Some 1300 enemy dead were claimed for the loss of 300 Americans, but the remainder of the enemy force managed to save themselves by retreating into Cambodia. Still, the 1st Air Cav had routed an enemy division which had threatened to cut South Vietnam in half.

In an attempt to provide enough U.S. troops to handle any NVA units in the country, thus leaving ARVNs free for actions against the VC, many more American troops were committed in late 1965 and in early 1966. This decision, which had been urged by Westmoreland, made sense since the greater mobility and firepower of the American units would enable them to fix and destroy the NVA units.

Among the other units arriving in the winter of 1965–6 and spring of 1966 were the 1st Infantry Division and 25th Infantry Division. So rapid was the build-up, in fact, that by the end of 1965, U.S. troop strength was over the 180,000 mark.

As Westmoreland's strength reached a level which permitted him to undertake more offensive actions. 'Search and destroy' tactics, in which U.S. troops swept an area in an attempt to bring enemy forces to battle or failing that to destroy their supplies, began to be widely used. These search and destroy missions were supported by artillery, often lifted in by choppers to form temporary fire support bases.

U.S. advisor to the ARVN Rangers wears the Rangers' very distinctive helmet cover bearing the black panther's head of the BDQs.

Continuing to show the value of airmobility, the 1st Air Cav in cooperation with ARVN, ROK (Republic of Korea), and USMC units started 1966 with Operation 'Masher/White Wing' which accounted for almost 2400 enemy casualties. Once again, the ability of the air cavalrymen to leapfrog troops and artillery support around the battlefield gave them an advantage over the Communist infantrymen. Two other important operations in the first half of 1966 – 'Hawthorne' and 'Paul Revere' – involved respectively the 1st Brigade, 101st Airborne Division and the 25th Infantry Division. Also during this period the 1st Infantry Division and the 173rd Airborne Brigade were used to weed out long established VC units near Saigon. By mid 1966, the military situation had been stabilized by the additional American troops, and the

threat of NVA units cutting South Vietnam in half was no longer present.

In summer and fall 1966, the 4th Infantry Division; the 1st Mechanized Brigade, 5th Infantry Division; 9th Infantry Division; 196th Infantry Brigade; 199th Infantry Brigade; and 11th Armored Cavalry Regiment arrived in Vietnam.

Among operations during later 1966 was 'Attleboro', the largest of the war up to that point. The 1st Air Cav also managed to stay busy during late 1966, proving the value of airmobility in Vietnam, and as a result were constantly involved in operations against enemy units. 1967 began with U.S. Army units involved in heavy operations throughout II, III, and IV Corps areas.

The scope of U.S. operations was increasing in 1967, and so was the enemy body count. The 1st Air Cav's operation 'Pershing' which began on 11 February 1967 and ran through January, 1968, would eventually account for 5401 enemy casualties. Two days after 'Pershing' began, the 9th Infantry Division along with ARVN and 'Ruff Puff' (Regional Forces and Popular Forces) units began 'Enterprise' which also ran through early 1968 and accounted for 2107 enemy casualties. And on 22 February 1967, the largest operation to that point in the war – 'Junction City' – was begun by elements of the 1st, 4th, and 25th Infantry Divisions, 196th Infantry Brigade, 11th Armored Cavalry Regiment, and 173rd Airborne Brigade, men from which undertook the only U.S. airborne assault of the war as part of this operation. 'Junction City' was centered in Tay Ninh Province but overlapped in bordering provinces and eventually accounted for 2728 enemy casualties.

During the second half of 1967 additional U.S. reinforcements arrived, including the 23rd (American) Infantry Division, the remainder of the 101st Airborne Division (which was converted to the second airmobile division in 1968), the 11th and 198th Infantry Brigades.

Shortly after arriving 'in country' two brigades of the 23rd Infantry Division began the year long operation 'Wheeler/Wallowa' in Quang Nam and Quang Tin Provinces which eventually resulted in more than 10,000 enemy casualties. Other major operations in late 1967 included 'Saratoga' by the 25th Infantry Division. Also late in 1967, U.S. intelligence agencies noticed a large increase in border clashes between infiltrating VC and NVA regulars and patrolling U.S. troops. These clashes, including large-scale ones involving the 1st Infantry Division, and the increased infiltration were harbingers of the coming Tet offensive.

In many ways 1968 marked the high tide of U.S. forces in Vietnam. During that year troop strength peaked at almost 550,000. In 1968 also VC strength was virtually broken as a result of heavy losses suffered during the Tet Offensive. Unfortunately, U.S. newsmen, for the most part, viewed Tet only superficially and emphasized the Communist attack on the U.S. Embassy or Communist activities in major cities rather than the staggering number of VC killed by the U.S., ARVN, and allied troops. As a result, many Americans at home were left with the misconception that Tet was a U.S./Vietnamese defeat rather than a resounding victory.

To appreciate the impact of the Tet Offensive, one must understand that in Vietnam the Lunar New Year (Tet) Holiday 29–31 January is perhaps even more significant than Christmas in Christian countries. As a result, the Communists hoped to achieve a surprise at least as thorough as the Germans had during the Ardennes Offensive. The battles along the border of South Vietnam which had begun in late 1967 continued in the first weeks of 1968, at least partially in hopes of pulling American troops away from key cities.

Fortunately for U.S. and ARVN troops, the Communists in one area attacked one day early telegraphing their punch. Even more fortunately, many of the cities attacked such as Ban Me Thuot and Nha Trang had heavy concentrations of U.S. Special Forces and MIKE Forces who were quick to respond.

In all, 36 provincial capitals were struck during Tet. The heaviest assaults were on Saigon, Quang Tri City, Da Nang, Nha Trang, Qui Nhon, Kontum City, Ban Me Thuot, My Tho, Can Tho, Hue, and Ben Tre. Although ten provincial capitals were temporarily captured by the VC (NVA regulars were only involved in any numbers in the northern province), they were soon regained.

Militarily, the Communists had suffered a crushing defeat. Out of the 84,000 Communist assault troops, 40–45,000 were killed, while another 7000 were taken prisoners.★ U.S./Allied and ARVN losses totaled 4314 killed and 16,063 wounded.

The first half of 1968 found U.S. troops helping to mop up the VC and NVA attackers during the Tet Offensive and also engaged in other operations throughout the country.

Members of 173rd Airborne Brigade set off smoke bombs to identify their position for spotter planes during Operation 'Macarthur'.

Members of the 9th Infantry Division crossing a stream in the Cam Sen area. The rear infantryman carries the AN/PRC25 radio with receiver thrown over his shoulder, and an M18 smoke grenade attached to his pack frame. It was very common practice for radiomen to carry M18s in this position.

New units arriving in 1968 included the 1st Mechanized Brigade, 5th Infantry Division and the 3rd Brigade of the 82nd Airborne Division. In July, 1968, Gen. Creighton Abrams took over as MACV Commander from Westmoreland.

Many of the operations began early in 1968 continued during the year, with U.S. and ARVN successes being marked throughout the country, even in IV Corps which contained the Mekong Delta, previously avoided by large U.S. Army units. 'Speedy Express', however, was mounted beginning in December of 1968 and extending until May, 1969, by the 9th Infantry Division in IV Corps. 'Speedy Express' resulted in almost 11,000 enemy casualties. It should be noted, by the way, that the author's recitation of casualty figures is not based on a penchant for statistics but on the fact that the primary U.S. objective was to fight a war of attrition against Communist forces. As a result, it became a 'body count' war.

Ironically, the North Vietnamese were also trying to inflict heavy casualties on the U.S. troops in hopes that the U.S.A. would lose its will to fight and pull out. Beyond a doubt the battle of attrition was being won by the heavier armed U.S. forces, but politically the nation was not willing to see the campaign through to the bitter end. One more comment on 'body count' is in order. Because of the difficulty in determining how one was performing in a guerrilla war, top ranking U.S. officers used the enemy body count as a barometer of success. Obviously, it then became advantageous for junior officers to achieve a high body count on operations. Hence, any enemy casualty figures not matched by nearly corresponding figures for weapons taken should have been suspect.

As previously stated, 1968 had marked the peak of U.S. involvement. The year 1969 saw the beginnings of 'Vietnamization' and the first reductions in U.S. troop strength. Although American troops still undertook operations in 1969, more stress was placed on beefing up ARVN units so that they could engage the enemy units themselves. Security duties previously undertaken by ARVN units were turned over to the 'Ruff Puffs'.

Another aspect of the war in 1969 was the conservatism of the NVA and VC. Tet as well as the many successful operations carried out in 1968 had given them a healthy respect for U.S. mobility and firepower. As a result, most large Communist units operated from Cambodia or Laos. Communist units within South Vietnam rarely exceeded platoon strength and were often only at squad strength. In response, U.S. units operated in small unit patrols on airmobile insertions into suspected VC/NVA lairs.

Despite the fact that U.S. Army units began to leave Vietnam in 1969 – the 9th Infantry Division less its 3rd Brigade pulling out in July and August and the 3rd Brigade of the 82nd Airborne leaving in September through December – U.S. Army units continued to be engaged in many operations, especially in the II and IV Corps areas. U.S. troop reductions continued in 1970. The 1st Infantry Division and the 3rd Brigade of the 4th Infantry Division left between February and April. The 3rd Brigade, 9th Infantry Division and 199th Infantry Brigade followed between July and October. And, between October and December, the remainder of the 4th Infantry Division and the 25th Infantry Division minus the 2nd Brigade headed back to the States.

U.S. offensive operations were limited during 1970, but in April–September a brigade of the 101st Airborne took part in 'Texas Star'. The major operation of the year, though, was the move into Cambodia to eliminate the safe refuge the NVA and VC had established there. Most of the ground troops moving into Cambodia were ARVNs, though U.S. advisors, artillery, and helicopters were heavily involved. Some U.S. ground units also took part in operations in Cambodia, including the 3rd Brigade of the ubiquitous 1st Air Cavalry Division and the 11th Armored Cavalry Regiment. U.S. helicopter gunships were especially important in giving support to the operations in Cambodia.

Actual enemy casualties inflicted were light, but large amounts of weapons and supplies were captured at Communist supply centers just over the border, and the ARVNs gained confidence in their ability to carry out offensive operations. Eventually, the other two brigades of the 1st Air Cavalry also became involved in the Cambodian 'incursion' as well.

The move into Cambodia had forced the North Vietnamese to rely even more heavily on the Ho Chi Minh Trail in Laos to supply their forces in the South. As a result, a cross border operation into Laos was planned to cut the trail. Congress had restricted the use of U.S. troops in Laos or Cambodia, so the operation was carried out by ARVN units. U.S. ground troops did participate, but 'theoretically' none crossed the Laotian border. Elements of the 101st Airborne Division (Airmobile), 5th Infantry Division, and 23rd

UNIFORMS OF THE INDO-CHINA AND VIETNAM WARS

Infantry Division provided support just inside the South Vietnamese border, and 600 U.S. helicopters gave the ARVNs airmobility and helicopter fire support. U.S. chopper losses were heavy – over 100, with hundreds more damaged – and the 'crack' ARVN units involved had to be hastily evacuated. 'Vietnamization' did not look as if it was working too well, but the U.S. troop reductions continued at an increasing rate.

Especially noteworthy was the fact that two units which had carried a heavy combat burden in Vietnam – the 1st Air Cavalry Division (less one brigade) and the 173rd Airborne Brigade – were pulled out during 1971. Also departing in that year were the 11th Armored Cavalry Regiment; the 2nd Brigade, 25th Infantry Division; the 23rd (American) Division (less some units); the 11th Infantry Brigade; the 198th Infantry Brigade; and the 101st Airborne Division (less some air cavalry squadrons); the latter of which began its withdrawal late in 1971 and completed it early in 1972. By the end of 1971, U.S. troop strength was down to under 150,000.

In Spring, 1972, the North Vietnamese began an invasion of South Vietnam, which with the assistance of massive U.S. air strikes and naval bombardments was repulsed. With the exception of advisors to ARVN units, few American ground troops were involved. Even during this enemy offensive, U.S. withdrawals continued, 24,000 American troops remaining at the end of 1972, only 16,000 of which were Army. The remaining air cavalry squadrons and the 196th Infantry Brigade were among units pulled out in 1972.

In effect, the U.S. Army commitment other than small advisory or logistical missions ended in 1972. Despite the unpopularity of the war at home and the difficulties in fighting a counter-insurgency war, U.S. Army units had performed well, consistently severely mauling NVA units which dared to engage them. Members of the U.S. Army won 155 Congressional Medals of Honor during the Vietnam war, almost two-thirds of them awarded posthumously. Heroism took other forms as well. Many soldiers in critical MOSs such as helicopter pilots volunteered for two or three tours of duty in Vietnam. Other Vietnam veterans viewing the U.S. pullout as a breach of faith begged to be allowed to return in 1975 to help prevent the fall of the Republic of Vietnam. Most of all, members of the U.S. Army knew the War was not lost on the battlefield but in the halls of government.

A breakdown of the units in which Medal of Honor recipients were serving at the time they performed their act of gallantry is indicative of the units seeing the heaviest combat in Vietnam.

1st Cavalry Division (Airmobile)	25
25th Infantry Division	21
101st Airborne Division	17
Special Forces	14
173rd Airborne Brigade	12
23rd (American) Infantry Division	11
4th Infantry Division	11
1st Infantry Division	11
9th Infantry Division	10
199th Infantry Brigade	4
1st Aviation Brigade	4
11th Armored Cavalry Regiment	3
All others	12

Airmobility

If any one concept is necessary to understand U.S. Army operations in Vietnam it is airmobility as applied to operations against the

U.S. ARMY

Tunnel Rat Tunnel rats were usually chosen because of their small stature to go into VC tunnel complexes to make sure that they were not still occupied. This was obviously a dangerous assignment. This 'tunnel rat' has removed his gas mask, though if the tunnel were still filled with CS gas it would be worn. Because of the heat and closeness in the tunnels, he wears only his trousers and jungle boots. A piece of OD towel or bandage is used as a sweatband. Only the 1911 .45 auto and angle-headed flashlight will be carried, though many tunnel rats also carried some type of radio; a miner's torch was sometimes used in lieu of the flashlight. His dog tag chain is worn inside of plastic tubing to prevent it turning green and from irritating his neck. A P38 can opener is also worn on the chain. **Helicopter Pilot** This pilot wears green utilities rather than the NOMEX flight suit, and black combat boots instead of jungle boots. Many aviators preferred the standard boot. His rank and branch insignia are subdued as is his First Aviation Brigade shoulder sleeve insignia. His locally made assault helicopter company pocket patch, however, is brightly colored. His mesh survival vest is half off, but the holster for his .38 Special revolver and some of the pouches containing survival radio, first aid kit, etc. are still visible. He carries the light aviation helmet in his right hand. **9th Infantry Division Grenadier** This 'grunt' has been slogging through the Mekong Delta. Tucked into the rubber band around his camo helmet cover are cigarettes and matches in a plastic case and jerky wrapped in foil. His vest is designed especially for grenadiers to allow the weight of extra 40 mm grenades to be evenly distributed. The butt and muzzle of his M79 grenade launcher are visible in his right hand. He wears the subdued 'cookie' 9th Division insignia on his left shoulder.

U.S. ARMY

Tunnel Rat

Helicopter Pilot

9th Infantry Division Grenadier

Air cavalryman of the 1st Air Cav guides in UH-1D 'slicks'
with his upraised M16 during Operation
'Wheeler/Wallowa'. Although the air cav usually traveled
light, these troopers carry full subsistence pack.

NVA/VC. The U.S. had begun experimenting
with the use of airmobile troops during the 1950s,
and in 1962 the Howze Board had recommended
that an air assault division be formed. The year
1962 also saw U.S. Army CH-21 Shawnee and
UH-1 Huey helicopters deployed to Vietnam.
The experiences of these chopper crews combined with the recommendations of the Howze
Board would help shape the airmobile division.
And, since operational experience of U.S. chopper pilots had been in Vietnam their recommendations led to the tailoring of a division especially
well-suited to the fighting there.

On 15 February 1963, the 11th Airborne
Division was reactivated at Ft Benning as the
11th Air Assault Division to test the concept of an
airmobile division. Initially, 3000 men were
assigned to the division, including a battalion-
sized infantry unit. Original aircraft complement
was 29 fixed wing and 125 helicopters. The 11th's
chopper pilots had to work especially hard to
learn formation flying. Many of them had, however, already gained combat experience in Vietnam and offered practical tips on using airmobility in combat. In late 1964, the 11th Air
Assault Division gave an impressive display of
tactical mobility against 'enemies' from the crack
82nd Airborne Division during 'Air Assault II'

maneuvers. So swift were the airmobile strikes
that the referees could not even keep track.

The 11th Air Assault Division had proven
itself, and there was a definite need for a highly
mobile striking force in Vietnam. Hence, on 1
July 1965, the 1st Cavalry Division was reactivated as the 1st Cavalry Division (Airmobile).
Incorporating the assets of the 11th Air Assault
Division along with troops from the 2nd Infantry
Division, 82nd Airborne Division, and 101st
Airborne Division, the 1st Air Cav prepared to
'mount up' for deployment to Vietnam, advance
units arriving at An Khe by 27 August.

Although the 1st Air Cavalry was the first
airmobile division in Vietnam it was not the first
U.S. Army unit to carry out air assaults there.
Both the 173rd Airborne Brigade and the 1st
Brigade, 101st Airborne Division, had already
been operating in the airmobile role.

As early as 1966, the Army began to suffer a
shortage of chopper pilots. Still, airmobility
assumed a greater and greater importance in
striking at the enemy. 'Skyhook' operations, in
which 'slicks' from Eagle Flights (consisting of
6–8 troop carrying helicopters [slicks], 5–6 Huey
gunships, and one flying ambulance) air assaulted into LZs right on the heels of their
gunships which softened up the LZ, proved
especially successful during 1966. At this point
the gunships were UH-1s armed with M60
GPMGs, 40 mm. grenade launchers, and 2.75
inch rockets.

Pilot shortages were not the only problem

facing the airmobile units. The choppers got so much air time that maintenance also became difficult. Much of this burden was relieved by the 'Corpus Christi Bay', a floating aircraft maintenance depot docked at Qui Nhon Harbor near An Khe where the 1st Air Cavalry Division was based. The 'Corpus Christi Bay' had 370 skilled technicians and files of 180,000 blue prints of aircraft systems. Using closed circuit TV these schematics or drawings could be projected for field maintenance units.

From the time the 1st Air Cavalry arrived in Vietnam, its units were in almost constant action. In just one operation – 'Crazy Horse' – 30,000 troops were moved by helicopter in a three week period. Air cavalrymen leapfrogged around the mountainous battle area to envelop the enemy while gunships overhead gave fire support with rockets. Eventually, they bottled up the 2nd VC Regiment, then unleash the B-52s and artillery.

Airmobile tactics developed 'in country' to meet situations as they arose. The 1st Air Cavalry literally functioned like the cavalry in western movies, arriving on the scene in their slicks in response to calls from Special Forces led CIDG units which made contact with the enemy. Techniques were also developed for landing troops where the tree canopy was too thick for LZs. Later, special LZ clearing bombs would be used, but in the early stages of the war, air cavalrymen descended via ropes or trooper ladders, or airmobile engineers would descend and clear an LZ with chainsaws and explosives.

9th Infantry Division members firing on enemy positions in a built up area. The left figure carries an M79 grenade launcher but also has an M72 LAW slung over his shoulder.

In 1966, the Army had reached the point where they were short 5000 aviators. To meet this ever increasing demand, the helicopter training school at Fort Rucker more than tripled its training load, many of the new chopper pilots being warrant officer graduates of the 32 week flight school.

By 1967, the 1st Air Cavalry's 400 choppers seemed to be constantly in the air as the air cavalrymen were called in again and again to fix and destroy enemy units. So successful, in fact, were Air Cavalry operations that the enemy withdrew north from Binh Dinh Province where the Air Cavalry was operating into Quang Ngai Province. Rapidly, air cavalry engineers built an airstrip at Duc Pho, and the 1st Air Cavalry Division moved into I Corps, previously a Marine Corps preserve, and continued to harry the NVA/VC.

To protect their base at Duc Pho during the hours of darkness, the air cavalry developed another airmobile tactic known as 'Night Hunter'. 'Night Hunter' ops involved four choppers. The lead Huey acted as a flare ship, dropping flares as it flew around the Duc Pho base area. The next two choppers were gunships whose door gunners swept the terrain below through starlight scopes, firing tracers if they spotted the enemy. The last chopper, another gunship, would then attack the enemy pinpointed with the flares using 2.75 inch rockets.

The air cavalry also made use of armed Chinook helicopters known as 'Go-Go Birds'. These helicopters carried two 20 mm. mini-guns, a 40 mm. grenade launcher, and .50 machineguns. Gunships were of immeasurable importance to the Air Cavalry, in effect fulfilling much of the function that artillery performed for regular infantry units. So far, however, the airborne artillery had been makeshift. In September, 1967, though, the first choppers designed strictly as gunships arrived in the Republic of Vietnam. These Huey Cobras (AH-1Gs) were armed with mini-guns, 40 mm. grenade launchers, 2.75 inch rockets, and late in the war TOW guided missiles. The Cobras also offered a much thinner profile than UH-1s, making them less vulnerable to ground fire.

In operations such as 'Pershing' late in 1967, the air cavalry also proved invaluable at cutting off enemy escape routes while ground troops moved in to herd the NVA or VC towards the air cavalry. Air cavalry choppers could even lift 105 mm. howitzers or 4.2 inch mortars into position ahead of the retreating enemy. A standard air cavalry tactic was to leapfrog artillery or mortars around the battlefield, leaving them in position only long enough to fire a few rounds. Just as the airmobile troops could be identified with the horse cavalry, this chopper-borne artillery was used much like the old horse artillery.

The air cavalry normally went into battle lightly equipped, relying on their choppers to bring in additional supplies as needed. The air cavalry also managed to avoid the 'bunker mentality' by constantly taking the war to the enemy. The air cavalry's ability to move fast and light and hit hard, their versatility, and their esprit de corps all proved invaluable during the Tet Offensive. Air cavalrymen air assaulted into positions behind the attacking NVA or VC units catching them in a murderous crossfire. Helicopter gunships were also important in the defense of many installations, including the key airbases of Tan Son Nhut and Bien Hoa.

Perhaps the best indication of the high regard in which Gen. Westmoreland held the 1st Air Cavalry Division can be gained from the fact that it was assigned a crucial role in breaking the siege of Khe Sanh. Again, the air cavalry's ability to leapfrog around the battlefield completely disorganized the Communist troops.

LRRP assigned to the 9th infantry Div. makes a commo check using the URC 10 emergency radio. The black beret was worn for a short time by the LRRPs in Vietnam, though normally not on missions. On the beret is a LRRP tab and the DI of the 9th Infantry Division. On his left breast this sergeant wears the combat infantryman's badge. His shoulder sleeve insignia is the subdued version of the 9th Infantry Div. 'cookie'. Above the SSI is an LRRP scroll. He also wears a locally made pocket patch.

Opposite:
U.S. Ranger advisors help train the ARVN Rangers at Duc My Ranger Training Center. Maroon beret was distinctive of the Rangers.

The 173rd Airborne Brigade and 101st Airborne Division were also operating primarily in the air assault role, the 'Screaming Eagles' being in the process of conversion to an airmobile division. The conversion began in July, 1968, and was completed about a year later. The 308th Aviation Battalion drawn from the 1st Aviation Brigade provided the basis for the 101st's aviation group.

During 1968, the air cavalry units also were used in III Corps to help stem infiltration from Cambodia. Chopper-borne patrols fanned out over three border provinces to sweep for infiltrating VC. Air cavalry interdiction proved relatively successful, though, of course, some VC made it through the net. Still, the enemy was forced to stockpile war supplies in Cambodia just across the border rather than risk bringing them into South Vietnam.

46

When U.S. and ARVN units moved into Cambodia in 1970, the 1st Air Cavalry Division played an important role in the operation, air cavalrymen being heli-lifted into many VC bunker areas. Air Cavalry gunships both supported the air assaults and shot up enemy complexes and trucks. In fact, the last unit to cross the border back into South Vietnam was a 1st Air Cavalry 'Pink Team' of one Huey Cobra gunship and one OH-6A (Cayuse) observation chopper.

By 1970 major U.S. airmobile operations had come to an end. During the years 1965 to 1970, the air cavalry had established themselves as a new battlefield elite and had proven a new mode of warfare. They had also helped American troops avoid the 'bunker mentality' which had played a part in defeating the French. The air cavalrymen kept on the offensive and always gave U.S. commanders flexibility of action. The Son Tay Raid had also shown that well-planned airmobile operations could be carried out deep into enemy territory.

In Vietnam, the single most important weapon remained man, but the chopper and its use in air assault tactics was the most important tool.

Uniforms and Equipment

Headgear worn by the Army in Vietnam was as diverse as the various combat arms involved. In the field, infantry, engineer, airmobile, and airborne troops normally wore the M1 steel helmet with camouflage cover. This cover had slits for the insertion of foliage, etc. for additional camouflage, and these slits often got torn in use. The rubber band which passed around the base of the helmet was often used for storage of 'bug juice' (insect repellent), cigarettes, matches, or

Machine-gunner from the 9th Infantry Division mans a .50 caliber MG with a 'Starlight' scope for night target acquisition.

Two men of the 196th Light Infantry Brigade fire at a VC position on a search and destroy mission near Tay Ninh in September, 1966. The man firing the M60 GPMG uses an asbestos glove.

other small items. The helmet liner could be worn under the helmet or on certain occasions, such as when mounting an honor guard, by itself.

Also popular in the field were the floppy bush or 'Jones' hats, in olive drab and in camouflage. Among special units such as the LRRPs, Ranger patrol caps or OD bandages used as bandannas or headbands were frequently chosen over more conventional headgear. LRRPs also wore black berets at one point, though rarely on operations. Instead, ARVN camouflage berets were worn in the field if any beret was. For men assigned to staff or other office positions away from the 'line', the olive green garrison or side cap was worn with the tan Class 'A' uniform.

The AN/PRR9 helmet mounted receiver and AN/PRT4 handheld transmitter were used by platoon leaders to keep in contact with squad leaders; the range was about one mile.

A member of the 1st Infantry Division festooned with equipment. Note the M18 colored smoke grenades, and the ax and machete, both used more for hand-to-hand combat in Vietnam than the bayonet.

Among other special headgear was the fiberglass helmet – CVC – with attached radio gear worn by armor crewmen. Helicopter crewmen also wore the light aviation fiberglass helmet which had headphones and boom mike attached. The gunner on a Huey Cobra might also have sighting apparatus for TOW missiles attached to his helmet late in the war.

For most Army units, the green utility uniform consisting of four pocket jacket and trousers was standard throughout the war. By late 1965 or early 1966, the cotton jungle utilities with the distinctive bellows pockets on the jacket were in general use. In earlier versions there were exposed buttons at the pockets and epaulets of the jacket. Later versions had flaps covering the buttons and were made of ripstop fabric which had nylon filaments woven in with the cotton. Special units such as the LRRPs wore camouflage utilities of either 'Tiger Stripes' or the later leaf pattern. Some older leopard spotted fatigues were available for the LRRPs but were unpopular because they stood out in the jungle. It was also hard to get 'Tiger Stripes' which would

fit since they were primarily for the much smaller ARVNs and 'cidgees'. Some were, however, available through Special Forces supply channels. Even when the ripstop fabrics came into use, utilities took a real beating on extended patrols in the 'boonies' and the normal practice was to throw them away upon returning from a patrol rather than to attempt to mend and wash them. During the early part of the war, chopper pilots wore standard utilities, but after 1969 most switched to the fire resistant Nomex two piece flying suit.

Footgear either consisted of standard black combat boots or the fabric, leather, and rubber jungle or tropical boots. The earliest type of jungle boots had buckles at the ankle, but these were uncomfortable and did not wear well. Later versions of the jungle boots had nylon reinforcement at the ankles and an aluminum insole for protection against punji spikes.

Various types of body armor were widely worn. The earlier type was collarless, while later armor had a three-quarter collar. Both were of ballistic nylon construction and had pockets and

U.S. Ranger advisor and ARVN Ranger watch hand-to-hand combat training at the Ranger Training Center. U.S. advisor wears the Ranger beret in the correct fashion, though most U.S. advisors preferred to 'age' their berets in such approved fashion as wearing them into the shower. Pocket patch worn by the U.S. Ranger is the black panther head of the Biet Dong Quan. In the earlier stages of the war when this photograph was taken there was leeway in personal sidearms. Many Special Forces and Rangers favored .357 Magnum revolvers which may be what this Ranger is carrying. This photograph was taken before subdued name tapes came into use, hence the white name tape.

grenade loops. In limited use was the ceramic breastplate ('chicken plate') armor used by those such as helicopter door gunners who would not have to 'hump' the 25 lb (11.33 kg.) plate and who were exposed to heavy enemy fire.

Almost universally used except among special units was the M-56 pistol belt/harness. In 'fighting load' order, the buttpack and/or rucksack would be deleted and just the M-56 harness, pistol belt, universal pouches (each holding four M16 magazines), canteen cover with plastic canteen, and field dressing pouch at the left shoulder would be worn. Normally, the M7 knife bayonet was worn on the belt and the OO angle-headed flashlight on the harness; grenades – usually the M26A1 'frags' – were normally attached to the universal pouches. M34 'Willie Pete' (White Phosphorous) grenades were normally carried in the rucksack. M18 'smokes' in red, green, yellow, or violet were sometimes worn attached to the suspenders, but this method actually offered too much chance of a branch, etc. catching them. There was also a pouch specifically for carrying

Rangers undergoing training at the MACV Recondo School call in an exfiltration chopper. Both men wear leaf pattern camo, and the instructor who is standing has a signal panel in his hands.

were adopted to hold spare magazines or grenades. Bandoliers of spare ammunition were also worn and extra canteens were attached wherever possible, both because LRRPs might have to avoid sources of water while operating in enemy territory and because their Long Range Patrol Rations needed a lot of water added to be palatable. LRRPs also chose indigenous rucksacks since if glimpsed through the trees they would not immediately identify their wearers as American troops. For similar reasons, LRRPs often wore an NVA sweater or some other piece of an enemy uniform to temporarily confuse any NVA or VC who might catch a glimpse of them.

Net survival vests with pockets containing first aid and other survival items and having built-in knife sheath and handgun holster were often worn by helicopter crewmen and occasionally by members of special units.

The authorized unit insignia for wear on the left uniform shoulder sleeve during the Vietnam War were the full color ones. Many units in Vietnam, however, issued or allowed their personnel to wear the subdued black and green versions of the insignia. On 1 July 1970, this became the official practice throughout the Army. An extremely wide assortment of locally produced unauthorized insignia and shoulder tabs were also worn. These included early subdued versions of unit insignia and special tabs such as 'LRRP' or 'Dog Handler'. U.S. advisors assigned to ARVN units often wore ARVN insignia or badges as well. Other personnel wore pocket emblems, often of plastic.

Hundreds of distinctive insignia (DIs) were worn by battalion and larger units in Vietnam. Locally produced versions of these DIs were painted rather than enameled and were on thin sheet metal – usually brass. These are commonly known as 'beer can' insignia.

Primary individual weapons carried by the Army in Vietnam were the M16 rifle and 1911A1 automatic pistol. In the early stages of the war, the M14 rifle and M1 and M2 carbines were also used. M79 40 mm. grenade launchers and M60 GPMGs were other standard weapons, and the sight of 'grunts' with belts of ammunition for the M60 around their torsos – especially in airborne or airmobile units – was a common one in

M18s, but many troops preferred to use the bag for the M18A1 Claymore anti-personnel mine to carry grenades or ammunition. Of course, these shoulder bags were also widely used as intended to carry the Claymore mine which when detonated could fire 700 steel balls in a predetermined direction making it a very devastating area defense weapon. LRRPs and some other special troops liked the Claymore because it was a ready source of C4 explosive which they used for rapid heating of their rations. Officers, etc. also carried their holstered 1911A1 .45 automatic pistol on their belt. The cotton bandoliers in which M16 stripper clips were issued were also frequently worn to carry additional ammunition.

Once again, LRRPs or other special troops did not use standard webbed gear or rucksack. Usually, M-56 gear was retained, but canteen covers

Many U.S. officers, especially those assigned as advisors to ARVN elite units wore locally tailored uniforms. This camouflage jacket shows many custom features such as extra stitching and zippers. Note the subdued combat infantryman's badge, U.S. parachutist wings, and ARVN parachutists wings. Normally subdued wings and combat infantryman's badge were in white thread but these are in black. On the left breast is ARVN jump status indicator badge, and between the top and second buttons is the Vietnamese rank equivalent.

Opposite:
Member of 82nd Airborne Division uses a flamethrower with dampened towels around his head and over the flame thrower to fight the heat given off by the weapon.

Above:
Captain and men of the 173rd Airborne Brigade on a village search in the Republic of Vietnam. The captain prefers the firepower of an M16 over his .45 Auto.

Vietnam. With Army special units, the CAR15 short version of the M16 was popular. M3 'Grease Guns', 12 gauge riot guns, XM21 snipers rifles (silenced in some cases), and M203 grenade launchers mounted on the M16 rifle were all used by infantry, airborne, and airmobile units. Point men especially liked the fighting shotgun and, once the anti-personnel round became available, the M79. Army air crews carried Smith & Wesson .38 Special revolvers – usually Model 10s – with either 2 or 4 inch barrels. For 'bunker busting' the M72 LAW was an ever popular weapon which was used against any 'hard' target in Vietnam. Early in the war, the M20 rocket launcher was still widely used as well.

The most widely used radios at platoon or company level were the AN/PRC-10 and AN/PRC-25 (which replaced the PRC-10). Both were FM receiver/transmitters. Weight was about 26 lbs (12 kg.) and both were carried on a pack frame. The PRC-10 contained 170 channels, while the PRC-25 contained 920. LRRPs and other special units also used the URC-10 emergency radio.

Members of a mortar team preparing to fire their weapon. Both soldiers wear flak vests.

Black beret with winged dagger badge of the Provincial Recon Units.

Men of the 11th Armored
Cavalry, with an M551
'Sheridan' air portable
fighting vehicle.

Men of the 173rd Airborne
Brigade pinned down on a
hill. Note rubber bands
around the helmet cover as
a storage place.

4 U.S. Marines

Other than a USMC liaison officer who actively participated in the French evacuation of North Vietnam (Haiphong 1954), the earliest U.S. Marine Corps presence in Vietnam was a few advisors to the Vietnamese Marine Corps. By 1956, two USMC officers and one sergeant were advising the VNMC. They found that their most important task was building aggressiveness and esprit de corps and teaching VNMC officers the basics of logistical planning.

The VNMC was one of the first units committed to the fight against the Viet Cong, and by 1960, U.S. advisors were accompanying VNMC units into combat. Beginning in 1961, the U.S. Marines also began rotating officers and NCOs to Vietnam for periods of two to four weeks in the 'On-the-Job Training' program so that they could observe conditions in the war being fought there. In effect, Vietnam was being used as a field classroom for studies in counterinsurgency warfare. Most of these Marines came from the 3rd Marine Division in Okinawa.

In early 1962 more Marine advisors arrived as the U.S.A. began to increase the number of U.S. personnel in Vietnam. U.S. Marine advisors took part in every combat operation the VNMC was involved in during 1962, and many Marines held important MACV staff positions.

In April, 1962, Marine Medium Helicopter Squadron 362 was deployed to Soc Trang in the Mekong Delta. This squadron and its support elements were known as SHUFLY and consisted of 24 HUS (UH-34D) 'Sea Horse' helicopters, three OE-1 fixed wing aircraft, and one R4D transport aircraft. A total of 534 USMC and USN personnel were assigned to the SHUFLY unit. Within a week of arriving 'in country', Marine helicopters were flying missions in support of the ARVN 7th Division, ARVN 21st Division, and VNMC. The Marine chopper pilots developed their tactics to fit the combat situations they faced, including executing the first night helicopter assault of the war.

As with most other U.S. troops sent to Vietnam, the men of HMM-362 were only there on temporary duty and were replaced by another helicopter squadron – HMM-163 – at the beginning of August. In September, the SHUFLY unit began moving its base of operations to Da Nang in the I Corps area where contingency plans called for the USMC ground units to be committed if needed. Primarily, the Marine choppers would be operating in support of the ARVN 1st and 2nd Divisions and some ARVN Ranger battalions. HMM-163 flew its first combat mission in I Corps on 18 September in support of the ARVN 2nd Division. In May, 1962, U.S. Marine units including a regimental landing team, an A-4C attack squadron, and a helicopter squadron moved into Thailand to counter a Pathet Lao/North Vietnamese threat on that country's border. By July, it was obvious the Marine presence had deterred the Communists from entering Thailand, and elements of the expeditionary force began to be pulled out of northern Thailand. Though they were not committed to combat operations, the 3000 plus Marines sent to Thailand demonstrated the United States' willingness to defend Thailand, an important demonstration for limiting Communist expansionism.

During 1963, U.S. Marine advisors continued to serve with VNMC battalions, among other important contributions helping the Vietnamese Marines set up their own separate training depot at Thu Duc. During the coup which toppled President Diem on 1 November 1963, USMC advisors did not get involved though the units they advised did.

SHUFLY operations continued in I Corps during 1963, though another UH-34D squadron – HMM-162 – had replaced HMM-163 in January. HMM-162 was, itself, replaced by HMM-261 in June, and HMM-261 was replaced by HMM-361 in October. Between the three Marine helicopter squadrons, they had flown more than 30,000 sorties during 1963. Having been involved in many air assaults, they had also lost quite a few choppers. The fact that Marine pilots were being rotated in and out of Vietnam

USMC Major Gen. Lewis Walt inspects Marine unit during Operation 'Harvest Moon'. In the foreground are two of the unwieldy pack racks used by the Corps. Note GI shoulder holster for a .45 auto on the man with the camera.

for such short tours may seem inefficient in retrospect, but it did ensure the Marines of a large pool of chopper pilots with at least some combat flying experience. As some Marines were wont to say, 'It's the only war we've got, so we've got to use it to the utmost.'

During 1964, the USMC advisory unit continued to work closely with the VNMC, both organizationally and operationally, though it should be noted that even by early 1964, only 11 USMC officers and nine NCOs were serving with the VNMC. Later in the year these numbers were increased by a few additional officers, but

the U.S. Marines were still strictly advisors.

Other Marines serving in Vietnam included the 30-man detachment at the United States Embassy, which unlike Marines on most such assignments might be expected to deal with attacks from VC terrorists. There were also USMC communications specialists serving in various capacities in Vietnam. Some Marine

Recons and intelligence and counterintelligence specialists also served short tours in Vietnam in 1964. Later in the year, USMC advisors who had previously just been serving with the VNMC were assigned to ARVN units in I Corps as well.

Major USMC operations continued to be carried out by the SHUFLY helicopter squadron which had a strength of 450 men in early 1964, but plans were that the 24 helicopters would be turned over to the VNAF on 30 June 1964 and the Marine pilots and groundcrewmen would be pulled out. Helicopter operations during early 1964 were primarily med evac and resupply runs, though during breaks in the monsoon some troop lifts were undertaken. In February, HMM-364 took over from HMM-361. As part of their duties, the men of HMM-364 began training VNAF pilots and groundcrewmen to take over from them since they were scheduled to be the last Marine helicopter squadron sent to Vietnam.

Because of VC sniping and other incidents around the base area at Da Nang, a Marine infantry platoon was deployed there for security in March, 1964. These 53 men from the 1st Battalion, 9th Marine Regiment, were limited to security duties around the base.

Beginning in April as the monsoon ended, the Marine helicopter crews began seeing their share of action as they were called on to provide airmobility for operations throughout the I Corps area. In fact, as the June departure date grew near, it was decided that the SHUFLY unit was still needed in South Vietnam. As a result, HMM-364 was ordered to turn its choppers over to the Vietnamese pilots on schedule, but a new USMC helicopter squadron – HMM-162 – was also deployed to Vietnam with its choppers. By the beginning of July, HMM-162 was ready to start flying missions.

Another new squadron – HMM-365 – replaced HMM-162 during the first week in October. One interesting innovation which occurred in November was the modification of three of the Marine UH-34Ds into gunships armed with the TK-1 system consisting of externally mounted M60 MGs and 2.75 inch rocket launchers. Also in November, the USMC security force was increased to company strength with 255 men from Company L, 3rd Battalion, 9th Marine Regiment as well as engineers, 81 mm. mortar teams, and a counter-mortar radar unit replacing the platoon previously on duty. HMM-365 saw quite a bit of action, and by the end of the year had already flown 6700 sorties.

At the start of 1965, various Marine units were in position for deployment to Vietnam, including the 9th Marine Expeditionary Brigade. As it turned out, however, the 1st LAAM (Light Anti-Aircraft Missile) Battalion was ordered to Da Nang first on 7 February. The 1st LAAM Battalion's HAWK missiles were felt to be a desirable adjunct to Da Nang's defenses in case the North Vietnamese launched air strikes in retaliation for the 'Flaming Dart' retaliatory strikes which had just taken place in the North. Finally, on 7 March, the two battalion landing teams (BLTs) of the 9th Marine Expeditionary Brigade received their orders to land at Da Nang with the mission of providing security for the base there. The 3rd Battalion, 9th Marine Regiment was landed amphibiously, and the 1st Battalion, 3rd Marine Regiment was airlifted to Da Nang. Other Marine units, including HMM-163, were placed under the operational control of 9th MEB commanded by Brigadier General Frederick Karch.

Other units arrived in Vietnam over the next week or so, including another helicopter squadron – HMM-162 – and by 23 March, 9th MEB strength stood at 4612. This included brigade logistic, engineer, and artillery support groups.

Once started, the USMC build-up in the I Corps area continued at a rapid pace. The 2nd Battalion, 3rd Regiment, arrived at Da Nang on 10 April, as did VMFA-531, a Marine F-4B squadron. By 20 April, 9th MEB strength had almost doubled to 8607. All were still at Da Nang except one battalion and some helicopters based at Phu Bai.

On 22 April, U.S. Marine ground units saw

U.S. General Insignia
First row, left to right: 114th Assault Helicopter Company patch; 191st Assault Helicopter Company patch; 1st Air Cavalry LRRP's (Long Range Reconnaissance Patrols) patch, sometimes known as the 'Horse Blanket' because of its large size. *Second row:* patch worn by USAF personnel involved in the Son Tay raid; 'KITD/FOHS' ('Kept in the Dark/Fed Only Horse Shit'); Rep. of Korea Capital Division (the 'Tigers') shoulder patch; patch worn by B-52 crews flying out of Anderson AFB, Guam (red represents North Vietnam, green South Vietnam, mailed fists of SAC are crushing letters 'V' and 'C'); *Third row:* MACV Recondo School graduates' 'beer can' distinctive insignia; 7th Transportation Bn 'beer can' distinctive insignia; 101st Airborne Div. LRRP's patch; *Fourth row:* patch worn by air crews who flew strike missions over North Vietnam (red line represents the Red River, the mount Thud Ridge, the star Hanoi); USN SEAL Teams breast badge; USMC Recons parachutists wings sewn directly on the Tiger Stripes camo.

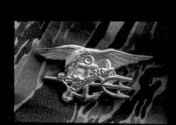

Although originally designed as a tank killer, armed with six 106 mm recoilless rifles, the Marines used the ONTOS in the infantry support role in Vietnam. Note the type of helmet worn by the Marine armored crewmen.

their first combat supported by VMFA-531. By the first week in May, the III Marine Expeditionary Force (the name of which was soon changed to III Marine Amphibious Force so it did not sound 'colonial') commanded by Major General William Collins had taken over responsibility for USMC units in I Corps from 9th MEB. III MEF headquarters was at Da Nang.

During the summer of 1965, Marine ground units undertook more operations. Marine aviators – both of fixed wing strike aircraft and of helicopters – also were heavily involved in operations by June. Also in June, Major General Lewis Walt, who was destined to be the most widely remembered Marine general of the war, took command of III MAF. During the summer, Chu Lai became an important Marine base, second only to Da Nang in size and importance.

Among aviation units arriving in June and July, either as replacements or added strength, were VMFA-513 and VMFA-542 with F-4s.

In August, the largest USMC operation to that time – in fact, the first U.S. regimental sized combat operation since the Korean War – took place when Operation 'Starlite' was launched south of Chu Lai. Marines from three battalions – 1/7th, 2/4th and 3/3rd – took part in this search and destroy operation which resulted in over 700 enemy casualties. August also saw USMC strength in I Corps rise to over 30,000.

Among operations during later 1965 were 'Golden Fleece' which provided security during the rice harvest to deny the VC food, 'Blue Marlin', a USMC/VNMC joint amphibious assault near Tam Ky, and 'Harvest Moon/Lien Ket 18' north of Chu Lai which resulted in over 400 VC casualties.

As of 31 December, III MAF strength in Vietnam stood at 39,092 troops. Of this total, 22,464 were at Da Nang, 13,995 at Chu Lai, and 2354 at Phu Bai. USMC organization can some-

times be confusing since the Marines normally identify units by regiment rather than division. Since May, 1965, the 3rd Marine Division had been based at Da Nang as part of III MAF. Regiments assigned to the 3rd Division were the 3rd, 4th, and 9th. Other units of special interest which arrived in Vietnam during 1965 included the 3rd Recon Battalion and the 1st Force Recon Company. The Recons were the Marine long range reconnaissance and raiding units. The 3rd Tank Battalion, 1st Amphibious Tractor Battalion, most of the 12th Artillery Regiment, and the 3rd Anti-tank Battalion as well as assorted other artillery units were also 'in country' by the end of 1965 to give heavy weapons support.

During early 1966, the Marines continued to increase their strength in the I Corps tactical zone. The remainder of the 1st Marine Regiment arrived in January, and by May, the 5th Marine Regiment had also been deployed to Vietnam. The 1st Marine Division comprised of the 1st, 5th, and 7th Regiments became operational at Chu Lai in February under the command of

Officers from the 3rd Marine Regiment study surrounding terrain from their positions. The lieutenant, at left, is a forward air controller, and carries an M18 smoke grenade on his pistol belt, probably for signalling his unit's position if an air strike is called in. Note that rank insignia is worn on both collars.

Major General Lewis Fields. Additional ground units which arrived early in 1966 included the 1st Tank Battalion, 3rd Amphibious Tractor Battalion, 1st Recon Battalion, the remainder of the 11th Artillery Regiment, and the 1st Anti-tank Battalion.

The Marines were involved in many operations early in 1966, especially during March when they took part in 'Utah/Lien Ket 26' and 'Tezas/Lien Ket 28'. Both of these operations by elements of the 1st Marine Division were in conjunction with Vietnamese forces. Operation 'Texas' had relieved An Hoa, an ARVN outpost besieged by NVA regulars and Main Force VC.

Since the Marines had deployed quickly in force late in 1965 and early in 1966, fewer units arrived during the second half of the year.

Elements of the 26th Regiment from the 5th Marine Division were deployed to Vietnam and assigned to the 1st Division, and additional armored strength was added in November with the arrival of the 1st Armored Amphibian Company. Also in November the two Marine divisions shifted their bases of operations. The 1st Division moved to Da Nang, and the 3rd Division moved north to Hue. The 5th and 7th Regiments, however, remained at Chu Lai.

Some additional U.S. Marine units arrived in Vietnam in later 1967, but most were of battalion size or less. 'Prairie I' ended in January, but Operation 'Prairie II', undertaken by some battalions of the 3rd Marine Division, continued near the DMZ until March. During 'Prairie I and II' the fighting had been especially heavy around Con Thien, elements of the 3rd Marine Regiment seeing a lot of action. In Quang Nam and Quang Tin Provinces in the southern part of I Corps, Marines from the 1st Marine Division – especially the 1st and 5th Regiments – were involved between April and June in Operations 'Union' and 'Union II' which eventually accounted for 1500 to 2000 enemy casualties. Also in May in a prelude to the next year's events, skirmishing went on around Khe Sanh.

Lieutenant General Robert Cushman took over command of III MAF from General Walt on 1 June. Beginning in July, Leathernecks from 3rd Marine Division were involved in a continuing series of operations in northern I Corps along the DMZ. Commencing with Operation 'Buffalo' in early July and followed by Operations 'Hickory II', 'Kingfisher', 'Kentucky', and 'Lancaster' the 3rd Marine Division had battalion or larger sized units in action until 31 October as part of these operations. Once again Con Thien seemed to be a pivotal point, and men from the 4th Marine Regiment were heavily engaged there in September and October. Con Thien which was located near Khe Sanh was besieged at various times during the late summer and early fall, but the siege was effectively ended in November with Operations 'Scotland' and 'Kentucky'. These operations around Khe Sanh during later 1967 eventually netted almost 8000 enemy casualties.

Further south in Quang Nam and Quang Tin Provinces, the major operation in late 1967 was 'Swift' in September which resulted in over 500 enemy casualties. The 5th Marine Regiment was heavily engaged during Operation 'Swift'.

Regimental deployments at the end of 1967 were: 1st – Quang Tri, 3rd – Dong Ha, 4th – Hue, 5th – Da Nang, 7th – Da Nang, 9th – Dong Ha, 26th – Khe Sanh. Both the 1st and 3rd Anti-tank Battalions left Vietnam in December.

Early 1968 saw the Marines fighting massive enemy attacks on cities in I Corps – especially Hue – and fighting to prevent Khe Sanh from falling to Communist besiegers. Only one major new USMC unit was deployed to Vietnam during 1968. The 27th Marine Regiment arrived at Da Nang in February, but it departed six months later in September.

The battle for Khe Sanh began on 21 January and was followed on 30 January by the launching of the Tet Offensive. The only real NVA success during Tet in I Corps was at Hue where the 4th and 6th NVA Regiments and six VC battalions captured most of the city and held it throughout February. By the end of that month, three U.S. Marine battalions along with eleven battalions of Vietnamese soldiers and marines had recaptured Hue, killing up to 8000 of the enemy in Hue and the surrounding area.

The siege of Khe Sanh lasted until 14 April when Operation 'Pegasus/Lam Son 207' relieved it. Despite 'scare' stories in the U.S. press, there was really little chance of Khe Sanh falling with the massive U.S. air support (including more

U.S. MARINES

Sergeant The dress blues uniform was not commonly worn in Southeast Asia because of the climate, but this sergeant is either on embassy guard duty or sea duty aboard a carrier, battleship, or cruiser. After the early stages of the war, embassy duty Marines in Saigon generally wore combat gear, especially after Tet. His blue tunic with collar, shoulder sleeve stripes, front, and bottom piped in red and three vertical buttons on the cuffs is the standard dress item for enlisted Marines. The gold chevrons on scarlet are worn to denote rank. The single chevron on the sleeve denotes four years service. The light blue trousers with scarlet stripes are standard with this uniform. White service hat, belt, and gloves round out the uniform to give the appearance which makes Marine honor guards so impressive. His weapon is the M14 rifle. **Major General Lewis Walt** Major General (later Lieutenant General) Walt was probably the most widely recognized Marine general officer in Vietnam, and like most USMC generals, still looks like a fighting infantryman. He wears green herringbone utility uniform with stars on the collar to denote his rank. He also wears the standard steel helmet with camouflage cover. On his pistol belt are a 1911 .45 auto and double magazine pouch. Typical of Marine Corps general officers, Gen. Walt wears only standard issue equipment. **Infantryman ('Grunt'), Circa 1965** This Marine infantryman wears utilities with fatigue cap, which has the Marine Corps emblem stenciled on the front. The M14 rifle is carried with spare magazine pouches worn on the belt.

U.S. MARINES

Sergeant

Infantryman ('Grunt'), Circa 1965

Major General Lewis Walt, USMC

A very heavily laden 'grunt' from the 7th Marine Regiment during 1967, wearing a rubber band around his helmet with a bottle of 'bug juice' tucked into it, and an OD towel to keep the pack straps from cutting into his shoulders. This sergeant appears to have been issued a pistol since he wears spare .45 auto magazines on his belt. He wears a Ka-Bar on his left hip and appears to have a spare one strapped to his pack. The rather uncomfortable edge on the issue pack frame is plainly visible.

than 7000 sorties by the 1st Marine Aircraft wing) brought to bear on the attackers. In fact, the 6000 men of the 9th and 26th Marine Regiments along with supporting artillery and an ARVN Ranger battalion were tying down at times more than 20,000 NVA troops.

In the southern part of I Corps, the U.S. Army conducted many operations in 1968, but the Marines still found plenty of action, especially in the northern provinces. Operation 'Scotland II' began on 15 April and ran until February, 1969. This operation around Khe Sanh eventually resulted in over 3000 enemy casualties. Men of 2nd Battalion, 4th Marine Regiment saw especially heavy fighting during the attack on Dai Do. Other major Marine operations included 'Allen Brook' running between 4 May and 24 August in southern Quang Nam Province and 'Mameluke Thrust' running from 18 May through 23 October in central Quang Nam Province. These two operations resulted in almost 3000 enemy casualties. Among units involved in these oper-

ations were the 7th Regiment and – before its redeployment – the 27th Regiment.

As 1968 ended, regimental deployment was as follows: 1st – Da Nang, 3rd – Dong Ha, 4th – Cam Lo, 5th – Da Nang, 7th – Da Nang, 9th – Khe Sanh, 26th – Da Nang. Operations by the Korean 2nd Marine Brigade and U.S. Army 23rd Infantry Division in southern I Corps had allowed Marine strength to be deployed further north to combat the larger NVA units which had entered the country during the Tet Offensive and the siege of Khe Sanh.

1969 was the year the Marines began pulling out of Vietnam, but early in the year they were still involved in major operations. 'Taylor Common' had begun in December, 1968, and continued until March, 1969. In this operation, Marines from the 1st Division accounted for almost 1300 enemy casualties. Between 22 January and 18 March, the 9th Marine Regiment was involved in 'Dewey Canyon', a highly successful operation just north of the A Shau Valley which resulted in over 1300 enemy casualties. Beginning on 1 March and running until 29 May, the 7th and 26th Regiments were involved in 'Oklahoma Hills', an operation southwest of Da Nang which inflicted almost 600 enemy casualties. Later in May and early June, the 9th Regiment joined with elements of the 101st Airborne Division in 'Apache Snow' in western Thua Thien Province. The last regimental sized operation of the war for the Marines occurred between 21 July and 25 September 1969 when the 3rd Marine Regiment took part in 'Idaho Canyon' in Quang Tri Province.

The Marines had been among the first U.S. combat troops sent to Vietnam, and some of them were among the first U.S. units to leave. During July and August, the 9th Regiment departed, to be followed in October and November by the 3rd and 4th Regiments. Other units leaving in 1969 included the 3rd Tank Battalion, 1st Amphibious Tractor Battalion, 1st Armored Amphibian Company, 3rd Recon Battalion, 1st Field Artillery Group, and most of the 12th Artillery Regiment. The headquarters of the 3rd Marine Division left on 30 November after most of its components had already been redeployed. By the end of the year, all of the other major USMC units were based in the Da Nang area themselves preparatory to leaving.

During 1970, the Marines continued to mount patrols around Da Nang, and pilots from HMM-263 and other Marine aviation units continued to fly missions. For the most part, however, the USMC units remaining in Vietnam were biding their time until being redeployed. The 26th Regiment left in March, and the 7th left in October. The remaining armored battalions along with most remaining artillery and engineer battalions also left during 1970. By the end of the year, only the 1st Regiment and 5th Regiment, along with other units assigned to the 1st Marine Division such as the 1st Recon Battalion, 1st Force Recon Company, three artillery battalions, an engineer battalion, and miscellaneous other units remained in country.

By June of 1971, the remaining Marine units had left Vietnam. Only some advisors, liaison personnel, and embassy guards remained. The Marines were not, however, gone for good. In April, 1972, in response to the North Vietnamese invasion, almost 900 Marines from the 9th Amphibious Brigade were sent to Vietnam to furnish security at Bien Hoa and Nam Phong Air Bases and to protect U.S. personnel and civilians.

Over 4000 more Marines from 9th Marine Amphibious Brigade were ready for rapid deployment should they be needed.

Over 800 Marines from the 3rd MAB also supplied ground security during the evacuation of American embassy personnel, other American citizens, and Vietnamese employees of the U.S. government on 29 April 1975 just before the fall of Saigon. These troops were brought in by CH-53s. The Marines found the biggest threat they had to deal with was not the VC or NVA, but ARVN paratroopers who were either shooting at the evacuation choppers or trying to force their way aboard.

USMC Cobra gunships supplied suppressive

Recons from the 3rd Recon Battalion cross the Mong River during a sweep and clear operation. Unlike the Special Forces which wore many pieces of equipment unique to them, the Recons normally wore standard Marine Corps equipment. The man in the right foreground actually wears standard utilities with sweat stains, not camouflage.

Marines from the 9th Marine Regiment move into a
Vietnamese village during Operation 'Harvest Moon'. Most
wear branches tucked into their helmet covers for
camouflage but the man at right is satisfied with his camo
cover.

fire during the evacuation. The Marine security
force was not lifted out until everyone authorized
for evacuation had been heli-lifted out of the
embassy compound. By 0800 hours on 30 April
1975, the U.S. Marines had finally left Vietnam
for good. They had not, however, left Southeast
Asia. Just over two weeks later on 15 May, U.S.
Marines were sent in to rescue crewmen of the
U.S.S. *Mayaguez* which had been seized by the
Communist government of Cambodia. Eighteen
Americans died in the *Mayaguez* incident, but
the quick American reaction did illustrate the
U.S.A. will to protect its citizens, an important
object lesson when dealing with Communist
governments.

The Marines lost 13,019 men killed in combat
in Vietnam, and 88,594 were wounded. Some
idea of the heavy burden of fighting borne by the
Marines can be gained from comparing their
casualties with the Army's. With total personnel
in the country five times that of the Marine
Corps, the Army lost 30,702 men killed in action
and 208,576 wounded. Marine casualties were
about 40 per cent. of those of the Army. This
means that the Marines suffered casualties at

about twice the rate of the Army. This difference
can be explained in many ways. The Marines
were operating in I Corps which abutted on
North Vietnam and thus saw heavier action
against NVA regulars. The Marines were also
aggressive patrollers who relied on the 'ground
pounder' to flush out the enemy. Finally, the
Marines traditionally have a much higher percentage of combatants than the Army. The
Marines put more of their strength on the line
and less in support roles. Hence, they have a
higher percentage of troops likely to see action
and likely to take casualties. One other interesting statistic is that only 26 Marines were captured
by the enemy. Marines are not much for
surrendering.

During the Vietnam conflict, Marines won 54
Congressional Medals of Honor. A breakdown
by the regiment the recipient was serving in at the
time he performed his act of gallantry illustrates
which USMC units saw most action:

4th Regiment	10
9th Regiment	8
7th Regiment	7
5th Regiment	6
Recon or Force Recon	6
3rd Regiment	5
1st Regiment	5
All others, including aviation units	7

Marines from the 3rd Marine Regiment assault Hill 881 in April, 1967, carrying only the light rucksack and entrenching tool on their backs, and armed with the M16.

It should be noted that like the Army's Special Forces, the Recons were engaged in many dangerous missions in enemy controlled territory and hence a high percentage of Medals of Honor were awarded for the relatively small number of men serving in Recon battalions or force Recon companies.

Historically, the U.S. Marines have been sent where the fighting was toughest, and Vietnam was no exception. Flanked by the VC and NVA in Laos to the west and North Vietnam to the north, the Marines were the ones occupying the key blocking positions between the North and the South. To mount a successful invasion of the Republic of Vietnam, the NVA would have had to first go through the Marines. The Communists had been successful in picking away at French border outposts, and they tried this same tactic once again against the Marines. It did not work. Perhaps the greatest single indication of the importance of the USMC in Vietnam can be found not in what happened while they were there but in what happened after they were gone. When the Communist offensive rolled south in 1975, it was the easy victories in I Corps – the Marines' old stomping ground – that convinced the Communists to keep driving south to Saigon. With 75,000 U.S. Marines blocking their path would that drive have been successful? To quote John Wayne, 'Not hardly!'

Uniforms and Equipment

Before discussing Marine uniforms and equipment, a few general comments are necessary. Historically, the Marines have often been saddled with equipment such as the World War II Reising SMG which was outmoded or inefficient. With that same perversity which has always made them such formidable adversaries, the Marines almost seem to relish 'cruel and unusual' equipment as long as it is marked 'USMC'. Army tank men always said you could tell the Marine Corps armor because of the oil leaks. That may have been true, but when they were needed for fire support, they always 'answered the bell'.

The Marine 'hooch' was normally a lot more Spartan than the field 'accommodations' of other troops in Vietnam. (Interestingly enough, the South Koreans managed to create some of the best 'hooches' for themselves, not because the ROKs ran a soft operation, but because they took the trouble to build dry comfortable 'hooches' out of ammo cans and crates in their off duty hours.) Still, the Marines did take a certain interest in their field quarters. After all, in the

U.S. Marine Recon on patrol carrying a heavy load of equipment since he is on an extended patrol behind enemy lines, near the DMZ and Laotian border in 1967, and the antennas of the radios carried by the men in the center and on right.

Marines of the 4th Marine Regiment on an operation near Phu Bai wearing standard green utilities with green fatigue hat. Weapon is the M14 rifle.

midst of the battle for Khe Sanh, the Leathernecks found time for rat killing expeditions.

Marine uniforms did not offer much variety either, and they were often worn until faded almost white, but one could usually tell the Marines, whatever the uniform and however worn, because they wore it with pride. Marines had it drilled into them in boot camp that one earned the right to wear a USMC uniform and they believed it. One could even tell the Marines out of uniform on R & R in Bangkok or elsewhere. They were the ones who did not slouch. There were, of course, exceptions. After being on patrol in the 'boonies' for a while or in a bunker at Khe Sanh for a month, the average Marine looked disheveled and 'dog-assed' tired.

The Marines often have their own names for things, too. Hats, for example, might be 'lids' or 'covers' and shirts might be 'blouses', but for consistency, the usually accepted terms will be used for describing uniform items. In fact, a whole chapter could probably be devoted just to the slang terms in use for items of uniforms and equipment by the different branches of the U.S. armed forces in Vietnam. The side cap, for example, was known as a 'cunt cap' in the Air Force, while to the Marines it was a 'piss-cutter'.

The standard issue cap for the Marines was the olive drab cloth fatigue or utility hat with the Marine Corps emblem printed or stenciled in black on the front. Officers also wore rank insignia on the front of this cap. In many cases, the fatigue cap became so faded by the sun that it appeared light green or even white. With the tropical khaki uniform, the khaki sidecap was worn with USMC emblem on the left side and – for officers – rank insignia on the right side. For combat, the M-1 steel helmet with helmet liner was worn, normally with camouflage cover. Fewer Marines wore the rubber band around the helmet than did Army personnel, but it was not uncommon to see Marines with the band, especially circa 1969–70. Other headgear worn by at least some Marines included armored crew helmets – MC2 – with attached microphones and both jet pilots and light aviation helmets for aviators. Some Marine helicopter door gunners wore helmets very similar in appearance to football helmets. Advisors to the VNMC occasionally wore VNMC berets. Other Marine advisors or Recons wore camouflage or OD utility hats or boonie hats. Very rarely worn in Vietnam and then normally only by honor guards aboard USN ships, embassy guards, etc. was the white

dress service cap with USMC insignia on the front.

The standard USMC uniform throughout the Vietnam War was OD green utilities. By 1966, the Marines were receiving virtually the same jungle utility as the Army. Like the later issue Army utilities, Marine 'greenies' had hidden pocket buttons. USMC was printed in black on the lower left pocket. Note that this was not a tape which was sewn on but was printed on the fabric. The eagle, globe, and anchor insignia was also printed in black above this. Rank insignia were worn on both collar points of the utilities. The belt worn with the utilities was light khaki but had often been cleaned to a yellow color. The

Marine observation post at Khe Sanh – the Marine in the foreground wears his Ka-Bar at his belt and, like many 'grunts', has decorated his helmet with graffiti.

buckle was brass. Also worn with the utilities was an OD T-shirt, and often because of the heat in Vietnam, this T-shirt was worn in lieu of the utility shirt, especially under the flak vest.

Many Marines wore utilities even when assigned to staff duties, however, the tropical khaki uniform was also worn for non-line duty or for liberty in Da Nang or elsewhere. This uniform was worn with a khaki belt.

Camouflage utilities were not in wide use among the Marines until 1969 or later when the

In 1964, HMM-364 choppers landing under direction of the loadmaster who wears the old style Marine spotted camouflage and M1955 flak jacket; he carries an M1 or M2 carbine.

Marines, wearing flak jackets, landing at Da Nang in 1965 showing the unwieldy Marine pack frame and full pack.

leaf pattern camo utilities began to be issued. Earlier, some Recons and some flight personnel did wear them as did advisors to the VNMC or other Vietnamese units. Many of those who did wear camouflage uniforms used the World War II style Marine spotted camo, though some tiger stripes or other patterns were available. Helicopter door gunners, for example, frequently wore tiger stripes. Generally, Marine helicopter crewmen flew in utilities as did even some jet pilots, however, NOMEX flight suits did receive some distribution among Marine Corps pilots.

Though only worn by embassy guards, honor guards, sea duty Marines, etc., the dress blues consisting of dark blue coat and grey trousers with a red stripe should be mentioned. This uniform was worn with a white belt. Because of the temperature and humidity in Southeast Asia, even embassy or other ceremonial guards rarely wore this uniform, however.

One other 'uniform' worn by a few Marines is worthy of mention. USMC marksmanship standards have always been high, and the Marines placed great emphasis on the use of snipers in Vietnam. Many of these Marine snipers developed their own versions of what some call 'ghillie suits' to hide themselves from the enemy. Usually, these sniper's outfits were made by cutting up vari-colored strips of canvas or other material and affixing it to shirt and trousers. Some type of snipers camouflage cape or head covering was also normally constructed to be worn.

As with most items, the Marines lagged behind the Army in receiving special footgear and made do with their black combat boots for the first years of the war, though by 1967 or 1968 jungle boots were being fairly widely issued to Marine units. Low quarter black dress shoes were worn with the tropical khaki uniform or dress blues.

Normally, the Marines did not use the M-56 harness as part of their load carrying gear, though Recons, other special troops and quite a few 'grunts' 'promoted' a set. The Marine light combat load was usually carried on the M61 OD webbed belt with OD suspenders which crossed in back to distribute the weight. Canteen, magazine pouches (each of which held one M14 magazine), grenades, knife, first aid kit, and – if carried – pistol holster could be carried on this belt. The Marines also used their own body armor – M1955. This 10 lb (4.5 kg.) vest consisted of 22 overlapping fiber glass plates. An 8½ lb (3.8 kg.) girdle, also known as 'armor-plated shorts', was issued but almost never worn except

Two U.S. Marine Recons wearing the camo helmet cover
in an interesting way, converted into a field camo beret.
Note the M3 'Grease Gun'.

Above:
Major Gen. Lewis Walt talking with members of the 7th Marine Regiment. Note the M14s and combination of helmets with camo covers and fatigue hats.

Left:
Marine artillerymen at Khe Sanh during the siege of that outpost wear Marines' M1955 flak jacket – note the grommets at the bottom for attaching equipment directly to the jacket.

Right:
U.S. Marines aboard a chopper preparing to land at Hue airport. The door gunner wears 'tiger stripes' camouflage and a football style helmet.

occasionally by helicopter crewmen who were concerned about fire from below hitting them in the 'privates'. The M1955 vest had grommets so that knife sheath, pistol holster, canteens, and other gear could be attached directly to the bottom of it. Spare magazines were usually carried in bandoliers around the waist or over the shoulder when the vest was worn.

Full Marine field equipment – '782 gear' – included an incredible array of items. The Marine pack frame was one of the most uncomfortable imaginable, and other than radiomen few 'humped' it in combat if they could avoid it. Among equipment issued was: haversack, knapsack, blanket, shelter half, poncho, tent pegs, ridge pole, guy line, extra boots, extra socks, extra underwear, spare uniform, mess kit, shaving kit, entrenching tool, and two canteens (the Marines retained the older metal canteen for much of the war). In practice, the 'grunt' usually only carried his green poncho, mess kit, en-

trenching tool, first aid kit, spare magazines, knife, grenades, and canteen (with Halizone tablets) in combat. Most Marines in the field used the light rucksack instead of the butt pack which was worn on the pistol belt. Rations were often carried in spare socks which were tied somewhere about the ruck or other equipment. Officers additionally carried their pistol, field glasses, maps, and compass. One practice followed by the Marines and other grunts in Vietnam was to wear a P38 can opener attached to their dog tags so one was always available.

On their utilities, marines normally wore only rank insignia. Officers insignia was the same as for the Air Force and Army, though there were some differences in insignia for warrant officers and enlisted men. A Marine Warrant Officer-4 insignia had three small red bars on silver, W-3 had two large red bars on silver, W-2 had three small red bars on gold, and W-1 had two large red bars on gold. For wear on the utilities, enlisted insignia was normally black metal, and for the tropical khaki uniform it was green on khaki cloth. A sergeant major wore three chevrons and three rockers with a star in the middle, a master gunner sergeant three chevrons and three rockers

Marine from the 5th Marine Regiment on an operation south of Tan Ky during June, 1967, equipped with the M16 and wearing only his OD T-shirt without his utility shirt. Instead of the Marine Ka-Bar knife he carries a Randall fighting knife.

Marines from the 9th Marine Regiment emplane to return to Okinawa after deploying to Thailand in 1962. Only rucksacks are worn. The man in the right foreground wears World War II style clip ammo pouches for the M1 Garand with which these Marines still appear to be armed.

with a grenade in the middle, and a first sergeant three chevrons and two rockers with a diamond in the middle. Ranks from master sergeant down to lance corporal wore insignia bearing chevrons or chevrons and rockers with crossed rifles. A Pfc wore just a single chevron. Very few locally produced insignia were worn by the Marines, but certain Recons did have a special parachutist's insignia made up consisting of a single wing and one-half of a parachute joined to one-half of a skull. Parachute qualified personnel, pilots, etc. sometimes wore subdued versions of their qualif-ication badges on utilities. Pilots or parachutists wings etc. were worn in silver on the tropical khaki uniform. Ribbons were also worn on it.

For the most part, the Marines used the same basic weapons as the Army with a few marked exceptions. Most Marines were issued the excell-ent Ka-Bar Bowie style fighting/survival knife. This traditional Marine blade was popular for all sorts of tasks while in the boonies and was also a

good hand-to-hand combat weapon if needed. The Marines also retained the M14 rifle through-out the Vietnam conflict. Most Marines were eventually issued M16s, but in some battalions the M14 was still favored. By 1968, most Marine units would be encountered using the M16, but a few retained their M14s until redeployed. In some Marine platoons, the M16 was issued, but the M14 was retained as a squad automatic weapon. Marine snipers used Winchester Model 70 and Remington Model 700 bolt action rifles with telescopic sights.

The Marines were especially fond of the M72 LAW, putting it to good use against VC bunkers. Other widely used Marine weapons included the 1911A1 Colt auto (though Marine aviators norm-ally carried .38 Special S & W revolvers in shoulder holsters), the M79 grenade launcher, M2 .50 MG, M60 GPMG, M19 60 mm. mortar, M29 81 mm. mortar, M40A1 106 mm. recoilless rifle, and the 3.5 inch rocket launcher.

Most widely used communications equipment by field units were the PRC-10 radio on a backpack (and which occasionally worked!), and the EE-8 field phone. The PRC-25 radio was issued to some Marine units before they left Vietnam.

5 U.S. Navy

During the French Indo-China War the U.S. Navy maintained liaison officers with the French and normally had naval forces patrolling in the South China Sea, but major U.S. Navy involvement in Indo-China did not begin until after the Geneva Accords in July, 1954, when American ships were used to move civilians who wanted to leave North Vietnam for South Vietnam.

To help train the personnel of the South Vietnamese Navy which was still in its embryonic stages, a small detachment of U.S. Naval personnel was assigned to the Naval Training Center at Nha Trang by early in 1955. During 1955 and 1956 American advisors continued to train Vietnamese sailors as part of the TRIM Program. In 1956 additional American Naval personnel, especially supply and logistics specialists, were sent to Vietnam to help the Vietnamese Navy absorb the equipment and supplies left by the departing French.

In June, 1956, a U.S. Naval task force – including the carrier *Yorktown* – was alerted to support the South Vietnamese against possible Chinese Communist incursions in the Paracel Islands. As it turned out, however, no Chinese troops were present on the islands. During the remainder of the 1950s the U.S. Navy's role in South Vietnam remained an advisory one. In December, 1961, however, U.S. ships began to patrol in conjunction with South Vietnamese ships off the coast of Vietnam, and in February, 1962, air patrols of the Seventh Fleet began covering the Paracel Islands.

During 1963 U.S. carriers were constantly on station off the Vietnamese coast. Among the missions performed by pilots from the carriers were reconnaissance missions along the North Vietnamese coast. More than one VFP-63 pilot was shot down flying these recon missions. U.S. Navy Seabees also began building camps in South Vietnam for the U.S. Army's Special Forces during 1962.

In May, 1964, Naval pilots from Seventh Fleet carriers began flying reconnaissance flights along

Members of a SEAL unit prepare to be put ashore on a raiding or ambush mission. Note the camouflage paint used on the faces and the diversity of headgear. In addition to two different types of camo boonie hats, two men are wearing the OD headscarves favored by the SEALs. Note also that the man at the lower right wears a vest for carrying 40 mm grenades, probably for the M203 launcher attached to the M16 rifle.

the Ho Chi Minh Trail in Laos. Later on 2 August 1964, North Vietnamese torpedo boats attacked the USS *Maddox* in the Gulf of Tonkin. One attacker was sunk and the other was driven off with the aid of F-8E aircraft of VF-53 from the carrier *Ticonderoga*. Again on 4 August

USN SEAL Team member eating 'C-rats'. He has added a cigarette pocket to the top of his camo boonie hat.

(Seabees) arrived 'in country' to build air bases and other facilities for the Marines and to undertake other construction projects. Almost all were assigned to the I Corps area. Naval corpsmen and chaplains were also serving with the 9th Marine Amphibious Brigade and other Marine units.

The U.S. Navy's primary task, however, remained to patrol the coasts of North and South Vietnam, giving fire support and providing air power in conjunction with the USAF. Naval aircraft played an important role in the renewed strikes against the North as part of 'Rolling Thunder'. To meet these many demands, by June the Navy had five attack carriers operating in the South China Sea.

The Navy also began patrolling Vietnamese waterways using P-2 Neptune, P-3 Orion, and P-5 Marlin aircraft as part of Operation 'Market Time'. Swift patrol boats and other types of patrol craft were also assigned to 'Market Time' operations. Plans were made during 1965 to deploy a U.S. Navy riverine force for operations in the Mekong Delta. In May, 1965, a destroyer – the USS *Henry W. Tucker* – was the first USN ship to be called upon to give gunfire support to troops in South Vietnam.

As part of 'Iron Hand' operations naval aircraft were involved in strikes against SAM sites in North Vietnam during the fall of 1965. A-4Es from the carrier *Independence* carried out the first successful anti-SAM strikes on 17 October 1965. MiGs had begun to attack aircraft over North Vietnam in April, 1965, and the first two MiGs were shot down on 17th June. By the end of 1965 carrier based aircraft had flown about 57,000 combat sorties.

At sea in October, 1966, Operation 'Sea Dragon' began in which American ships interdicted North Vietnamese coastal traffic. The Navy also increased its participation within the Republic of Vietnam substantially with the commitment of men from SEAL Team One in February to aid in the counterinsurgency campaign in the Mekong Delta. The SEALs, who took their name from the three elements they were trained to operate – Sea, Air, Land – were the Navy's elite special warfare troops, and they proved especially valuable at intelligence gathering and at mounting three man hunter/killer operations against the VC out of bases at Nha Be, Binh Thuy, and My Tho. The SEALs were especially effective at ambushes and made the Rung Sat Special Zone a hazardous place for the VC to operate. Deployment of U.S. riverine

Communist torpedo boats attempted to attack U.S. destroyers in the Gulf of Tonkin. In retaliation on 5 August aircraft from the carriers *Constellation* and *Ticonderoga* attacked the Vietnamese torpedo boat bases, destroying or damaging up to 25 enemy PT boats.

Later in 1964 Task Force 77 was enlarged even more with the addition of two more carriers – the *Ranger* and the ASW (anti-submarine warfare) carrier *Kearsage*. During February, 1965, additional carrier strikes were launched against targets in North Vietnam in retaliation for attacks on U.S. installations in South Vietnam.

As part of the U.S. troop build-up in Vietnam during 1965, six Mobile Construction Battalions

forces to the Mekong Delta began when PACVs (patrol air cushion vehicles) and 'Seawolf' helicopters commenced operations in mid-1966 in support of the SEALs.

Naval air strikes against North Vietnam did not recommence after the Christmas, 1965, bombing halt until February, 1966. One of the most successful raids took place on 18 April when two A-6s from VA-85 of the *Kitty Hawk* hit the Uong Bi power plant which supplied one-third of North Vietnam's electrical power, putting it out of operation. Beginning in April, Naval pilots were assigned coastal targets, while the Air Force was assigned inland targets. A-4s of VA-153 and VA-155 from the *Coral Sea* became expert 'truck busters' along the Ho Chi Minh Trail in 1966.

Other important Naval air successes in 1966 included the destruction of the Hai Duong

USN doctor treats a Vietnamese child; with USMC officer, ARVN captain at left and ARVN LTC next to him. Note the ARVN Ranger badge on the captain's left breast; he wears the standard ARVN infantry beret.

Bridge in August by an A-6. Strikes against North Vietnamese petroleum and industrial complexes also began in June, 1966, aircraft from *Ranger* striking oil-storage facilities at Haiphong for the first time on 29 June.

In 1967 River Assault Flotilla One began large scale operations on Vietnamese waterways in the Mekong Delta in conjunction with troops from the U.S. Army 9th Infantry Division. The River Assault Flotilla included such craft as monitors, armed troop carriers, assault support patrol boats, and command and communications boats. Naval helicopters were also assigned to the flotilla as were men from the SEAL teams.

Working closely with the riverine forces, SEAL Teams One and Two continued their operations during 1967. In addition to raiding VC 'safe' areas the SEALs set up long term surveillance posts along VC supply routes. SEAL ambushes were so successful during the year that many VC supply routes were virtually shut down for fear of the SEALs.

As of December, 1967, there were 18 Naval Mobile Construction battalions 'in country' as the Seabees were called on for all sorts of construction tasks.

Just as the USAF pilots were frustrated by restrictions placed upon their attacks on the North, so were the Navy pilots. Still, Navy pilots continued to strike against the Communists.

Early in 1968, Naval air strikes were used in tactical support of Marine defenders of Khe Sanh. In February and March, for example, 3100 sorties were flown in support of Khe Sanh's defenders by carrier based aircraft. At the end of March President Johnson ordered a halt to bombing north of the 20th Parallel. Naval aircraft continued flying missions in southern North Vietnam and Laos until all bombing in North Vietnam was halted in October.

During 1968 the riverine war continued with operations by naval units around My Tho, Ben Tre, Cai Lay, Cai Be, and Vinh Long during the Tet Offensive. The Mobile Riverine Force reached a strength during the year of four river assault squadrons with almost 200 craft. A whole series of 'Coronado' operations during 1967 and 1968 had denied the VC use of coastal waterways, and 'Sea Lords' operations from November, 1968 through January, 1969 resulted in over 2500 enemy killed in action as well as hundreds of tons of enemy supplies captured.

Though the SEAL teams worked with the Mobile Riverine Force they also continued their raids, ambushes, and surveillance missions. SEALs also performed underwater demolitions to open river channels for riverine patrol craft. In addition, the SEALs began working closely with the PRUs (Provincial Reconnaissance Units) assigned to the Phoenix Program in 1968, and the combination of the SEALs and the PRUs proved deadly to the VC hierarchy in the Mekong Delta.

By 1969 the U.S. Navy's riverine forces were already beginning to turn their craft over to the Vietnamese Navy, though U.S. Naval craft and crews continued to be involved in 'Sea Lords' operations in the early part of the year. On 1 February, 25 river assault craft of River Assault Division 91 were transferred to the VNN. Still, 160 U.S. Navy river assault craft remained in operation during March. U.S. riverine forces were active in Kien Hoa Province during May, but in June, 64 additional river assault craft were turned over to the Vietnamese Navy. Diminished U.S. riverine forces continued to operate through the end of 1969, but by early 1970 operations had been turned almost entirely over to the Vietnamese.

Three SEAL Team One detachments – Bravo, Echo, and Golf – remained 'in country' during 1969, and they continued to operate primarily in the Mekong Delta, though some SEALs were also assigned to MACV/SOG or other special operations units. In addition to their normal raiding and ambush missions, in 1969 the SEALs played an important part in the Coastal Surveillance Force and in the 'Vietnamization' of the PRUs.

In early 1969 the carriers *Hancock*, *Kitty Hawk*, *Ranger*, and *Coral Sea* were on station off Vietnam. Naval air strikes during the first half of the year were primarily in the I Corps area of South Vietnam since the bombing halt against the North continued. There were occasional

---

U.S. NAVY

Lieutenant, Advisor to the Junk Forces Because the Junk Forces were frequently involved in boarding or landing operations, this officer is well armed with an M16 rifle and a .45 automatic pistol, the latter carried in a commercial rather than a GI issue shoulder holster. Utilities are olive drab with white name and 'U.S. NAVY' tapes. The utility hat is navy blue with rank insignia worn on the front. The equivalent VNN rank insignia is worn on his shirt flap in the center of his chest. **SEAL** Dressed for operations in the Mekong Delta, this SEAL wears the old style locally produced tiger-striped camouflage utilities. He wears the camo beret often associated with the SEALs and flopped over the left eye in Viet/French fashion rather than in standard U.S. fashion. His weapon is the Ithaca Model 37 'trench' shotgun. On his pistol belt he wears two GI shotgun shell pouches, each holding 12 extra rounds of 12 gauge buckshot or flechette ammo, two M26 'frags', and a Ka-Bar fighting/survival knife. His boots are standard jungle boots. Face and body camouflage paint is applied in the distinctive pattern associated with the SEALs. **Carrier Pilot** This naval aviator wears a flight suit (green and orange flight suits were also worn, though the latter was discarded when it was discovered how visible it made shot-down pilots to pursuing NVA). Over it, he wears a 'g-suit' and survival gear. He carries a strobe, .38 caliber revolver, .38 special ammo bandolier, and jet pilot's survival knife in pouches and, among other items, a first aid kit, sea biscuits, shark repellent, and signal mirror. He wears the tan side cap and carries his helmet with his name and squadron designation painted on. His boots are brown, standard with naval aviation personnel.

U.S. NAVY

Lieutenant, Advisor to the Junk Forces

SEAL

Carrier Jet Pilot

Members of a USN SEAL Team prepare to go ashore on an operation. Note the assortment of headgear, including an OD scarf on the man in the middle and the belt of ammo for the Stoner M63 LMG wrapped around the middle man.

strikes into the North in later 1969, mostly in retaliation for firing on U.S. reconnaissance aircraft.

Nine Seabee battalions had left Vietnam in 1969, and another six left during 1970 since new U.S. construction was virtually halted as U.S. troops left in increasing numbers. Except for some naval advisors and helicopter pilots, most of the riverine forces had left Vietnam by 1970, but SEAL Team One continued its operations. SEAL Detachment Bravo worked with the PRUs until March by which time the 'prews' were pretty well integrated into the National Police Field Force. SEAL Detachment Sierra acted as advisors to the Vietnamese SEALs during 1970. Although SEAL operations decreased, Navy Special Warfare personnel still carried out raids such as the one on 22 November, 1970, in which

15 SEALs helped free POWs from a VC prison camp. SEALs still carried out ambushes, too, though often they would go along as 'advisors' to the LDNN (Viet SEALs).

Naval air operations in 1970 were mostly ground support operations in South Vietnam or missions against the Ho Chi Minh Trail.

During 1971 naval airpower, especially from the carrier *Hancock*, was used in Laos in support of 'Lam Son 719'. Carrier pilots also flew some missions in southern North Vietnam during 1971. These were mostly either reconnaissance missions or retaliatory raids.

Beginning in 1972 air activity increased against North Vietnam as more protective reaction strikes were flown against SAM (Surface to Air Missile) and AA (anti-aircraft) installations.

By July, 1965, in fact, six carriers were operating in the Gulf of Tonkin, the maximum number on station at any time during the war. Aircraft from these carriers flew ground support missions for South Vietnamese forces and also flew missions against the North. On 8 May, A-6s from

three of the carriers mined Haiphong and other harbors for the first time, a move the Navy had been pushing for years.

Bombing north of the 20th Parallel was again halted in October, but when peace negotiations broke down 'Linebacker II' was launched on 18 December, 1972. Air Force B-52s carried much of the bombing load, though. On 12 January 1973 a fighter from *Midway* scored the last MiG kill of the war over the Gulf of Tonkin bringing the Navy's total to 59 confirmed MiGs downed.

On 23 January the cessation of hostilities was announced, and by the end of January Navy minesweepers were headed for Haiphong to help clear the mines dropped a few months previously. Naval and Marine helicopters also helped with the mine clearing operation. By the end of July the mine clearing had been completed.

Carrier air strikes continued against Communist targets in Cambodia and Laos during the first half of 1973, but by 15 August all American air strikes were halted.

As the fall of Phnom Penh had become immi-

USN SEAL Team members come ashore from a PBR.

nent in April, 1975, the *Midway* and *Enterprise* had been recalled to the South China Sea. *Coral Sea* and *Hancock* joined the other carriers in time for the evacuation of South Vietnam as the fall of Saigon approached. The new F-14 'Tomcat' from the *Enterprise* flew air cover along with A-7s and A-6s, while helicopters flew evacuation missions. Eventually, 8000 people were lifted out to the fleet offshore.

During the Vietnam War, 1093 members of the U.S. Navy were killed in action. Another 145 died of wounds. Eighteen died in captivity, and 266 are listed as presumed dead. Ten members of the U.S. Navy in Vietnam were awarded Congressional Medals of Honor: three medical corpsmen and a chaplain serving with the USMC; three with the riverine forces; a SEAL; a rescue helicopter pilot; and a seabee.

The most obvious contribution of the Navy during the war was, of course, massive air

USN riverine unit members taking part in operations along the Bassac River in the Mekong Delta wearing the flak jacket used by USN personnel.

support from carrier based aircraft. The carriers gave the U.S. great flexibility in deploying air power both strategically against the North and tactically against Communists in the South. Capital ships such as the battleship *New Jersey* or the cruiser *St Paul* both gave naval gun support and presented a massive interdiction threat off the coasts of Vietnam. Smaller craft carried the main burden of interdicting coastal traffic, but they were backed up by the CVs, BB, CAs, and CLs.

Although the Vietnam War abounded with special warfare troops, the Navy's SEALs are often rated the elite of the elites. Man for man the SEALs were probably the toughest fighting force in Vietnam, and they along with the U.S. Navy's riverine forces played a key role in wresting the Mekong Delta – long a VC sanctuary – from enemy control. Neither should the role of the Seabees be underrated. All or part of 21 Seabee battalions served in Vietnam and the airstrips, port facilities, or other important installations they built were absolutely necessary to support the American war effort.

Uniforms and Equipment

Probably the most well known U.S. Naval headgear is the white 'Dixie Cup' cap worn by enlisted personnel. This cap was worn both at sea and ashore during the Vietnam War, but was not universally worn by personnel actually serving in the Republic of Vietnam. Standard Naval officers hat was the service hat in either white or khaki. Aviators sometimes wore a green service hat. A khaki garrison cap was also worn by officers.

Both enlisted personnel and officers sometimes wore a baseball style dark blue utility hat with rank insignia affixed to the front. Aircraft carrier flight deck personnel wore 'crash helmets' of various colors which designated their assigned duties. Some naval personnel assigned to shore duties – especially the Seabees – wore USMC green fatigue hats. Many naval personnel assigned to the riverine forces adopted the black beret of the Vietnamese Navy's junk force. SEALs favored a distinctive camouflage beret but also wore camo boonie hats or just OD scarves or head bands.

Among Naval officers the most common uniform worn in Southeast Asia was the tropical working uniform consisting of a khaki shirt without a tie and khaki trousers. Officers also wore the dungaree working uniform consisting of a light blue denim shirt and dark blue denim trousers. Green fatigues of USMC pattern were sometimes worn as well, especially by officers assigned to Seabee or riverine units. Rank insignia was worn on both collars.

Among enlisted personnel the most commonly encountered uniform aboard ship and ashore was probably the dungaree working uniform. Green fatigues were also worn by riverine personnel and Seabees. For shore leave in Bangkok, Hong Kong, etc. dress whites, consisting of bell bottomed pocketless trousers and white sailor jumper with sailors tie, were worn. Special personnel

wore special uniforms. SEALs normally wore camouflage utilities – usually tiger stripes, though sometimes local cammies or utilities dyed black were used. For underwater missions khaki swim trunks with a wet suit top were standard. Aircraft carrier flight deck crews normally wore pullover sweaters or jerseys of different colors to designate their assignments: for example – yellow – plane directors ; blue – elevator operators and plane handlers; green – catapult and arresting gear personnel; brown – plane captains; and red – ordnancemen and firefighters. Naval aviators wore green flight suits with white jet pilots helmets.

The standard naval dress shoe was black, but officers wore white dress shoes with their summer 'whites'. In actual Vietnam service USMC

Men of Light Helicopter Attack Squadron Three of the USN riverine forces, wearing the black berets.

combat boots, and, later, jungle boots were more common. SEALs and riverine personnel often wore sneakers as did some sailors aboard ships, though for shipboard duties black low quarter shoes similar to the dress shoes were also sometimes worn. Aviators and aviation ratings wore brown shoes, for which reason naval aviators were known as 'brown shoes'. SEALs and UDTs, of course, wore flippers while undertaking many of their combat swimming assignments.

Naval officers rank insignia were similar to those of the other branches but had naval designations. Five stars worn in pentagonal arrangement designated a fleet admiral, four stars an admiral, three stars a vice admiral, two stars a rear admiral, and one star a commodore (a virtually extinct rank). A captain wore a silver eagle, a commander a silver oak leaf, a lieutenant commander a gold oak leaf, a lieutenant two silver bars, a lieutenant (jg) a silver bar, and an ensign a gold bar. These were the insignia normally worn on the khaki uniform or the fatigues. On dress uniforms Naval officers wore a series of wide and narrow stripes at the cuff to designate rank.

Warrant officers, of which there were four classes – W-4, W-3, W-2, and W-1 – wore either three or two silver bars on a blue enamel background for W-4 and W-3 respectively or three or two gold bars on the same background for W-2 and W-1 respectively. Petty officers wore chevrons with an eagle over crossed anchors. A master chief petty officer wore three chevrons with a rocker and two stars above the eagle, a senior chief petty officer the same with one star, and a chief petty officer the same with no stars. Petty officer first class wore three chevrons with no rocker or stars, petty officer second class two chevrons, and petty officer third class one chevron. A seaman wore three half chevrons. Rating insignia varied in color by specialties. Seamen wore white on blue, Seabees light blue, and airmen green. Among badges worn on the white or khaki uniform for officers were aviators wings consisting of a winged anchor and shield, small craft (riverine) badge consisting of an anchor with a small boat and three stars above, and the special warfare (SEAL) badge consisting of an eagle, trident, anchor, and flintlock pistol. Some of these badges existed in an officers and enlisted version. Officers versions of the small craft and special warfare badges were gold and enlisted men were silver.

Naval riverine personnel normally carried Colt 1911A1 .45 automatic pistols. Standard handgun for naval aviators was the Colt or S & W .38 Special revolver, but some S & W Model 39 automatics were also issued. The SEALs had their own version of the S & W 9 mm. – the Mark 22, Model O – which was fabricated of stainless steel so it would not rust and which was silenced.

A special subsonic 9 mm. round with a rubber 'O' ring was used in this weapon. Thompson SMGs, M3 'Greaseguns', M1 and M2 Carbines, and M16s were all used by riverine units, with the M16 becoming standardized by 1968. The SEALs favored the Stoner M63A1 LMG in 5.56 mm. caliber with a 150 round drum magazine. SEALs also used the M16 or CAR15 and the

USMC Naval Gunfire Team plots a mission for an offshore ship. Two of them wear boonie hats; figure at left appears to wear a camo fatigue hat, though it may just be sweat stained.

Ithaca slide action 12 gauge shotgun. Reportedly the SEALs used some of the special 12 gauge flechette loads issued to the Marine Corps in their Ithacas. The M79 grenade launcher was a popular weapon with both the SEALs and the riverine units, though the SEALs actually preferred the M203 launcher mounted on the M16. Normal armament for a three man SEAL ambush unit was one M16 (often with an M203), one Stoner M63A1, and one Ithaca shotgun, SEALs also carried either the U.S. Navy Underwater Knife, a Ka-Bar, or some other fighting knife such as a Gerber or Randall.

6 U.S. Air Force

Since World War II, the United States has put great stress on the use of air power in any conflict, and Vietnam was no exception. Actually, U.S. Air Force pilots and mechanics served in Vietnam during the French Indo-China War, and a U.S. B-29 raid was considered as a means to support the defenders of Dien Bien Phu. As with so many decisions in the Vietnam Wars, this one was based on politics, and the B-29 strike did not take place.

After an independent Republic of Vietnam was created, U.S. Air Force personnel acted as advisors to the Vietnamese Air Force (VNAF). Throughout the 1950s, a small number of USAF officers and technicians helped the VNAF keep their obsolete planes flying and to learn to fly the new equipment which the U.S.A. began to supply in 1960.

In 1961, President Kennedy sent a detachment of the 507th Tactical Control Group to Vietnam to establish a radar warning station at Tan Son Nhut Air Base near Saigon. Also in 1961, General Curtis LeMay, architect of Strategic Air Command and then Chief of Staff of the Air Force, established the 4400th Combat Crew Training Squadron (also known as the 'Jungle Jims') which was in reality an air commando unit specializing in COIN (counterinsurgency) operations. In December, 1961, this unit was deployed to Vietnam. Four RF-101s were also sent to Tan Son Nhut in 1961 to fly recon missions over Vietnam and Laos.

Many other USAF units were deployed to Thailand during 1961 as well, and in November, 1961, a brigadier general was placed in command of the USAF units in Southeast Asia which by then also included a squadron of C-123 (Ranch Hand) defoliation planes.

To upgrade their fighter capability, the VNAF received 30 T-28s, and in January, 1962, USAF pilots started training the Vietnamese to fly these aircraft. Night flying was stressed, and U.S. pilots flying SC-47s started dropping flares to light up targets for VNAF strikes. This technique was also taught to the Vietnamese pilots.

Air Policeman checks civilian employee at Tan Son Nhut in 1967. Note the distinctive 'AP' helmet, badge, etc.

Another high priority in early 1962 was helping the Vietnamese set up a better air control and warning system. The USAF, still primarily as advisors, became more involved in ground support missions and in supplying Forward Air Controllers (FACs) to ground units in summer

85

USAF Pararescueman – note white flight helmet and maroon beret tucked into the zipper pocket of the flight suit. A panel on the left breast of the flight jacket bears both aircrewmans wings and parachutists badge; on the right breast is the patch of the Aerospace Rescue and Recovery Service.

and fall of 1962, and by late that year, more American planes were on request for assignment to Vietnam. Some of these aircraft were needed to augment the VNAFs transport capability. Thirty USAF pilots were also assigned to fly VNAF C-47s so that some Vietnamese pilots could be transferred to flying T-28s.

By January, 1963, it looked as if increasing demands on the VNAF were going to stretch it too thin so General Anthis, CO of USAF units in Southeast Asia, asked for one USAF T-28 squadron, one USAF B-26 squadron, two RF-101 reconnaissance planes (in addition to four already 'in country'), and two RB-26s for photo reconnaissance. Two additional C-123 transport

squadrons were also requested. Seemingly as if to back up these requests, ARVN forces suffered a defeat in the Battle of Ap Bac because they lacked proper air support. In April, one of the C-123 squadrons requested was sent to Vietnam, and in July the U.S. 19th Tactical Air Support Squadron was activated at Bien Hoa. The lack of well-trained VNAF FACs and of a good air-to-ground communications system still hampered operations, however. USAF T-28s based at Soc Trang were called on especially often to provide air cover and ground support for ARVN operations in the Mekong Delta, but they were stretched so thin that they could only respond to some of the requests.

The summer of 1963 marked the point at which the 4400th Combat Crew Training Squadron began operating under its true colors, redesignated 1st Air Commando Squadron.

Since the U.S. Air Force's part in the Vietnam conflict was growing, command of the 2nd Air

Division which controlled most USAF assets and personnel in Vietnam was taken over on 31 January 1964 by Major General Joseph H. Moore. Still, however, the intention was to pull out USAF units as soon as the VNAF was capable of functioning on its own. U.S. pilots continued to fly missions, though, but by April, losses – due more to the T-28s' age than enemy action – were taking their toll of the 2nd Air Division's effectiveness.

In May, 1964, U.S. pilots were ordered to stop flying combat missions and to limit themselves to training VNAF pilots. USAF personnel also continued to work with the VNAF to coordinate ground support so that it arrived in time to help ARVN units under attack.

The USAF's low key role in Vietnam suddenly changed on 2 August 1964 when North Vietnamese torpedo boats attacked U.S. ships in the Gulf of Tonkin. In retaliation, President Johnson ordered U.S. Naval aircraft to attack naval bases on the North Vietnamese coast, and two USAF B-57 squadrons were sent to Bien Hoa and fighter squadrons flying F-100s and F-102s were sent to Da Nang. More fighters were deployed to bases in Thailand as well.

On 1 November 1964, the vulnerability of air bases in South Vietnam was graphically illustrated when VC mortar squads shelled Bien Hoa, killing four Americans and wounding seventy-two. Five B-57s were destroyed and 15 damaged. Partially as a result of this attack, on 2 December President Johnson approved air strikes against the enemy infiltration routes in Laos.

Some USAF units were now flying A-1E Skyraiders, and in December these units along with VNAF Skyraiders hit the VC hard.

On 7 February 1965 VC mortar attacks on the advisor's compound at Pleiku killed eight Americans and wounded more than a hundred. Tuy Hoa airfield was also attacked. In retaliation, air strikes were launched against North Vietnamese facilities.

B-57s were also used against VC base camps near the Cambodian border on 19 February, and B-57s and F-100s were used again two days later to give support to a Special Forces led CIDG unit which had been ambushed along Route 19. Even more importantly, February was the month which saw two B-52 squadrons deployed to Anderson AFB, Guam. To increase ground support effectiveness, in February the USAF activated four Cessna O-1 squadrons as FACs.

SP stands guard at Cam Ranh Bay Air Base, carrying the short version of the M16 – the CAR15 – standard issue for dog handlers who normally carried it with the sling affixed to the top of the weapon, as does this SP, so that the weapon could be carried slung in the ready position over the right shoulder. The SP could bring his weapon into action while still controlling his dog's lead with his left hand. When an 80 lb attack trained German shepherd 'alerted' there was no chance to use both hands on one's weapon. A .38 special S & W revolver was normally carried on the right hip.

The real USAF offensive against North Vietnam began on 2 March with the launching of 'Rolling Thunder'. On that day, the NVA ammunition depot at Xom Bong was nearly destroyed by 25 F-105s and 20 B-57s. The 'Rolling Thunder' campaign was to be carried out under strict geographical limitations to keep the war from widening, however. Any target attacked in North Vietnam needed prior Presidential approval, and to help select targets U-2 planes began

USAF Pararescueman on a jungle penetrator, wearing camouflage utilities, helmet, and jungle boots.

flying over North Vietnam in April. Originally, VNAF planes were involved in the strikes against North Vietnam, but they soon limited themselves to providing air support to ARVN forces in the South.

As 'Rolling Thunder' continued, attacks moved progressively further north. The first target above the 20th Parallel to be attacked was the barracks at Quang Soui which was hit by USAF F-105s on 22 May 1965.

On 18 June, the B-52s got into action for the first time as 30 'Buffs' (Big, Ugly, Fat Fellas) from Strategic Air Command's 3rd Air Division flew out of Guam to attack a VC base area in the Ben Cat Special Zone north of Saigon. This was the first of the B-52 'Arc Light' missions which

gave ground support by attacking enemy troop concentrations.

On 23 July 1965, a USAF F-4C was shot down by a North Vietnamese SA-2 missile. As a result, SAM sites became fair game for the 'Thuds' which began attacking them a few days later. Special 'Iron Hand' missions with the primary objective of eliminating as many SAM sites as possible began in August, but the sites in the Hanoi/Haiphong area were still off limits for air strikes. Another method for dealing with the SAMs developed in 1965 was the use of F-105s in the 'Wild Weasel' program. These aircraft were equipped with Shrike missiles which homed in on the SAM radar if it was turned on. The pilots needed any breaks they could get, too, because political restrictions forced them to fly in certain air corridors which the North Vietnamese knew about and could target SAMs, AA, and MiGs on.

In late 1965, B-52s also began striking the Ho Chi Minh Trail, each one carrying up to a hundred 750 lb (34 kg.) bombs. USAF strength 'in country' increased at a rapid pace too. In October F-100 squadrons were deployed to Bien Hoa and Da Nang, and in November, F-4C Phantoms were based at Cam Ranh Bay. Also in that month, AC-47 gunships – 'Puff the Magic Dragon' – began flying out of Tan Son Nhut. By the end of 1965, there were 21,000 USAF personnel in the Republic of Vietnam and more than 500 aircraft. Many more men and planes were also based in Thailand.

During a U.S. bombing halt stretching from December, 1965, through January, 1966, the North Vietnamese repaired many roads and bridges damaged by 'Rolling Thunder' raids and continued to build SAM sites. Despite the bombing halt in the North, though, the USAF

Col. Jack Broughton (right) and another 'Thud' pilot showing off USAF flight suits, insignia, and 'baseball' and garrison cap.

continued to build up its strength in the South, adding two F-4 squadrons and an F-5 squadron early in 1966.

In April, 1966, the B-52s were authorized to strike into North Vietnam, and for their premier performance hit the Mu Gia Pass, an important access point to the Ho Chi Minh Trail.

Beginning in July, 1966, the Air Force gave special emphasis to striking at the North Vietnamese rail network in an attempt to slow the flow of war materials to Communist units in the South. Parts of the Ho Chi Minh Trail were also designated SLAM (Seek-Locate-Annihilate-Monitor) zones for B-52s. These were, in effect, free fire zones, and anything moving in them was fair game. Since March, 1966, 'Combat Skyspot', a sophisticated radar direction system, had been in operation at Bien Hoa, and this was especially helpful for the B-52s.

During Operation 'Attleboro' running from September through November, thousands of sorties were flown by the USAF, many of them close air support missions. In 'Attleboro' and countless other ground support missions during 1966, the airborne FACs proved invaluable at directing USAF strike aircraft to their targets. The combination of the AC-47 gunships and AC-123s armed with cluster bombs proved especially useful in attacking targets along the Ho Chi Minh Trail as well as in defending hamlets, Special Forces camps, etc. from night attacks.

'Rolling Thunder' operations continued through the end of 1966 at a heavy pace, September being the peak month with 12,000 sorties being flown. Over 100,000 sorties were flown during 1966. By late 1966, B-52s were flying 600 sorties per month. Also in 1966, the MiGs began to come up to meet the attacking aircraft, causing F-4s to be sent specifically for fighter cover.

Within South Vietnam, Operation 'Cedar Falls' was launched in January, and 1113 sorties were flown in support of it. Over 700 enemy dead were credited to the air strikes alone. An even larger operation – 'Junction City' – was launched in February, and more than 5000 tactical sorties as well as 125 B-52 sorties were flown in support of it. The USAF also either air dropped or airlifted almost 25,000 tons of munitions or supplies in support of this operation.

All through the first half of 1967, air attacks continued against the North with many new targets being hit, including the Thai Nguyen iron and steel plant near Hanoi. Beginning in April, B-52s began flying missions out of U-Tapao Royal Thai Air Base, thus granting them much more versatility in employment than when they were based only on Guam. NVAF planes did not come up to engage the attackers again until April of that year, but once again they suffered heavy losses. In May alone, USAF crews shot down twenty MiGs.

When NVA artillery began shelling bases just south of the DMZ in April and May, tactical air strikes were called in, and 30 NVA sites were put out of action on 16–17 May. Later in September, air power was used against NVA artillery sites shelling the Marine base at Con Thien.

In July even more targets were opened up for 'Rolling Thunder' attacks, many of them in the Hanoi/Haiphong area. On 2 August, the Paul Doumer Bridge, one of the most important rail and highway bridges in the North, was attacked for the first time and was severely damaged.

Despite losses inflicted on the MiGs in the first half of 1967, they became aggressive again in the latter part of the year, and permission was given for the first time to strike the MiG bases, driving most of the NVAF north to Chinese airfields. Air Supremacy was virtually complete over North Vietnam by the fall of 1967. During the year, 75 MiGs were downed by American crews, while 25 U.S. aircraft were lost in air-to-air combat.

As 1968 began, there were 56,000 USAF personnel in South Vietnam and thousands more in Thailand. One of the major uses of airpower in that year occurred at Khe Sanh where more than 24,000 tactical sorties and 2700 B-52 sorties were flown against the Communist troops surrounding that Marine base.

The 'Igloo White' system was activated in late 1967. After aerial reconnaissance, the best locations for seeding acoustic and seismic sensors along the Ho Chi Minh Trail complex were selected. A-1s, CH-3 helicopters, and F-4Ds were the primary aircraft used to deliver the sensors, which were camouflaged to look like everything from weeds to animal droppings.

U.S. AIR FORCE

Air Commando Captain This Air Commando wears a flight suit which he has altered by cutting off the sleeves. His name and pilots wings are worn on a tape over the left breast. His headgear is the distinctive Air Commando bush hat, always worn with one side turned up. His weapons are an AR15 adopted by the Air Force for the Air Commandos before the Army adopted the M16, and a S & W Model 15 .38 Special revolver on his left hip in cross draw position.

Security Police Dog Handler This SP wears late pattern tiger-striped utilities with a subdued Security Police badge on the left breast pocket. His headgear is the boonie hat used by all sorts of personnel in Vietnam. On his pistol belt he wears the USAF issue pouch for two 20 round M16 magazines, worn upside down so that the magazines will fall into the hand when the flap is opened. On his right hip he carries a S & W Model 15 revolver, spare ammo for which is carried in the two black leather six-round cartridge pouches over his right hipbone. His primary weapon is the CAR15 SMG version of the M16 slung in assault position.

Combat Controller This CCT wears leaf pattern camo utilities with the dark blue beret of the Combat Control Teams. Silver jump wings are worn as a beret badge. Functioning much as the Army LRRPs or the USMC Recons, this CCT carries a radio to call in airstrikes. Like the LRPP, he carries multiple canteens. His weapons are the ubiquitous – at least among Air Force personnel – S & W M15, the CAR15, and a Randall fighting knife. Ammo pouches are the same as those worn by the S.P.

U.S. AIR FORCE

Air Commando
Captain

Combat Controller

Security Police Dog Handler

Information from these sensors was fed into two giant computers at the Infiltration Surveillance Center at Nakhon Phanom Royal Thai Air Base supposedly the largest building in Southeast Asia, though because of the top secret nature of what went on there few knew about it. Security around it was tight, as around other 'hush hush' items at Nakhon Phanom such as the spy planes based there. As a result, Nakhon Phanom always had a large contingent of the Air Force's top Security Policemen assigned to base security.

'Igloo White' sensors had been in place along the Ho Chi Minh Trail since 1967, and AC-47s, A-26s, and AC-123Bs were all acting as truck busters using information supplied by these sensors to find their targets. Air Force C-123 and C-130 transports were also important in the defense of Khe Sanh.

Shortly after the siege of Khe Sanh began, the VC threw everything they had at the major population areas of South Vietnam during the Tet Offensive. Despite the demands on U.S. Air Force equipment and manpower made by the battle for Khe Sanh, thousands of sorties were also flown in support of U.S. and ARVN troops

during Tet. At Hue, for example, B-52s launched saturation raids against enemy forces. Air strikes were launched against enemy concentrations, even in Saigon itself, whenever possible during Tet. Once again the AC-47 gunships proved particularly valuable, especially in defending the Air Force's own facilities at Bien Hoa and Tan Son Nhut.

In early 1968, President Johnson imposed limitations on the 'Rolling Thunder' strikes against the North, first ordering a halt to bombing north of the 20th Parallel, and then north of the 19th Parallel. The raids below the 19th Parallel were primarily against the infiltration routes into South Vietnam and entrances to the Ho Chi Minh Trail.

As of 1 November, all U.S. air strikes against North Vietnam were halted in an attempt to work out peace terms. During 1968 the USAF had been plenty busy in South Vietnam, though, having flown 840,117 combat sorties in support of ground troops. 1968 also saw some important new equipment enter the USAF inventory. The OV-10 Bronco began service with FACs during the year, and laser guided 'smart' bombs came into use during 1968. June, 1968, was also the month when USAF fighter/strike aircraft strength reached the peak level in South Vietnam at 737. Another peak was reached when USAF personnel strength went over the 54,400 mark.

In 1969 'Vietnamization' began, but the Air Force was obliged to assume more responsibility rather than less to take up the slack as U.S. ground troops were committed less. Ground support missions were flown in support of major operations and in aid of Army and Marine Corps fire bases located in exposed areas.

Whenever enemy troop build-ups were detected, the Air Force was called in to hit the massed Communist forces. 'Commando Hunt III' was launched in November, 1969, against the Ho Chi Minh Trail. Stretching into early 1970, it was estimated that up to 10,000 enemy trucks were destroyed in these air operations against the 'Trail' during late 1969 and early 1970. AC-119 and AC-130 gunships along with C-123s equipped with bomblet canisters accounted for about half of this total. The USAF also flew many operations during 1969 – as it had for

U-10 Courier pilot from the 5th Air Commando Squadron checks equipment before flying a psychological warfare mission. He wears his net survival vest over his flak jacket and carries his S & W revolver.

USAF Deployments in Southeast Asia, July 1969.

VIETNAM

Tan Son Nhut	7th Air Force HQ, Air Force Advisory Group, 6250th Support Squadron, 834th Air Division HQ, 2nd Aerial Port Group, 377th Combat Support Group, 1964th Communications Group, 1st Civil Engineering Group, 505th Tactical Control Group, 3rd Aerospace Rescue and Recovery Group, 12th Reconnaissance Intelligence Technical Squadron, 460th Tactical Reconnaissance Wing, and 1st Weather Group.
Bien Hoa	3rd Tactical Fighter Wing, 504th Tactical Support Group.
Phan Rang	315th Special Operations Wing, 35th Tactical Fighter Wing.
Cam Ranh Bay	483rd Tactical Airlift Wing, 12th Tactical Fighter Wing.
Phu Cat	37th Tactical Fighter Wing.
Pleiku	633rd Special Operations Wing.
Nha Trang	14th Special Operations Wing.
Tuy Hoa	31st Tactical Fighter Wing.
Binh Thuy	632nd Combat Support Group.

THAILAND

Udorn	7/13th Air Force HQ, 432nd Tactical Reconnaissance Wing.
Ubon	8th Tactical Fighter Wing.
Takhli	355th Tactical Fighter Wing.
Korat Wing	388th Tactical Fighter Wing, 553rd Tactical Reconnaissance Wing.
Don Muang	631st Combat Support Group.
U-Tapao	635th Combat Support Group.
Nakhon Phanom	56th Special Operations Wing, Task Force Alpha.

the previous few years – in support of Gen. Vang Pao's Meos who were fighting the Pathet Lao and NVA in Laos.

In addition, the Air Force provided tactical and strategic airlift throughout Southeast Asia. Reconnaissance flights continued over North Vietnam, too, even though air strikes did not resume against the North in 1969. B-52 strikes against Communist sanctuaries inside Cambodia were, however, authorized in that year.

Pararescuemen check out their medical supplies prior to a mission. Note the maroon berets and the leaf pattern camouflage worn by the man on the left. The men at the center and right wear standard USAF 'greenies'. It took an order by the Flight Surgeon to allow long-sleeved uniforms to be worn with sleeves rolled up in SE Asia. The figure at the right wears flight crewman's wings above the 'USAF' tape.

In 1970, USAF personnel spent even more time training the VNAF to take over responsibility as USAF units began pulling out. Additional planes were added to the VNAF inventory and many additional pilots were trained.

Limited air strikes were again launched against the North when the North Vietnamese began firing at U.S. reconnaissance aircraft in 1970. These 'protective reaction' strikes were against SAM sites and AA installations.

Beginning in February, USAF B-52s began flying missions against Pathet Lao and NVA positions in Northern Laos in support of Mec and Laotian troops fighting there. Both tactical and B-52 strikes were also flown in large numbers during the 'incursion' into Cambodia when U.S. and ARVN troops moved across the border on 29 April, 1970.

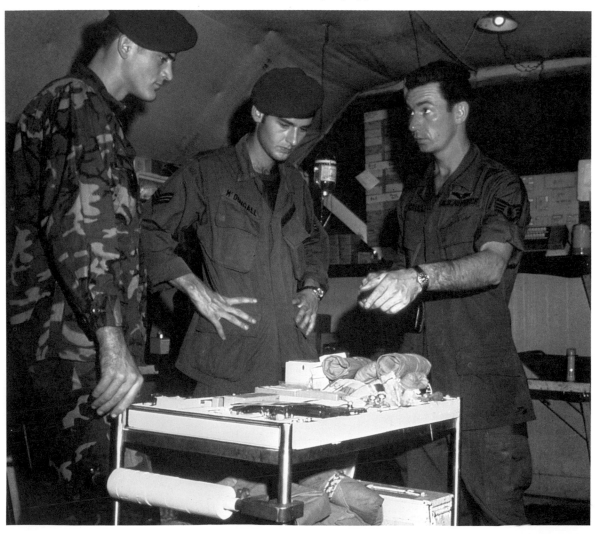

During 1970, the USAF flew 48,064 attack sorties. As an increasing indication of 'Vietnamization' the VNAF had taken up much of the slack, flying 28,249 attack sorties.

In February, 1971, ARVN units moved into Laos in an attempt to cut the Ho Chi Minh Trail in 'Operation Lam Son 719'. Although U.S. ground troops were not involved, USAF pilots flew ground support, FAC, reconnaissance, and transport missions during the Laos operation. AC-119 and AC-130 gunships also flew night fire support missions around ARVN positions, and C-130s dropped 15,000 lb (6804 kg.) bombs on suspected enemy troop concentrations. Between 14 and 24 February 399 B-52 sorties were made.

During the operation, the USAF flew more than 8000 tactical air sorties and 1358 B-52 sorties. Without U.S. air power 'Lam Son 719'

would probably have been a severe ARVN defeat. With the heavy air support, the ARVNs withdrew in relatively good order, although they had suffered heavy losses and the Ho Chi Minh Trail was not cut.

U.S. air power was still necessary in preventing the defeat of government forces in Cambodia as well. Just to keep supply routes open to Phnom Penh required massive air support.

During 1971, protective reaction strikes continued against SAM and AA sites in the North,

Aircrewman prepares to 'seed' an ADSID sensor along the Ho Chi Minh Trail. Note flight helmet, flight suit and standard USAF black combat boots. Both these heavy duty black boots and jungle boots were worn by USAF personnel. SPs, PJs, and CCTs especially favored the latter.

and there were also air strikes against infiltration routes just above the DMZ and against fuel storage areas south of Dong Hoi. MiGs began to prove a problem again late in 1971, and in November, USAF and USN planes struck at three MiG bases.

Commando hunt operations also continued against the Ho Chi Minh Trail in Southern Laos, but by 1971, the Communists had emplaced more than 300 AA guns along the Trail making attacks against NVA convoys more difficult. As a result, the use of laser-guided bombs, B-52s and B-57s, and AC-119 and AC-130 gunships locked into the 'Igloo White' computer system became more common during 'Commando Hunt VII' operations in late 1971 and early 1972.

By the end of 1971, the number of USAF strike aircraft in South Vietnam had dropped to 277, about one-third of the peak number, and USAF personnel were down 28,791, about one-half of the peak. These figures were somewhat misleading, since many units had not returned to the U.S. but had been reassigned to bases in Thailand.

In late 1971 and early 1972, an NVA build-up was detected just north of the DMZ, and hundreds of sorties were flown against targets in that area. On 30 March 1972, however, the Communists launched a massive invasion of the South from North Vietnam, Laos, and Cambodia. U.S. tac air and B-52 strikes were launched repeatedly against the enemy armor in an attempt to blunt the advance. More than 10,000 tactical air and B-52 sorties were logged just in support of the heavily outnumbered ARVN forces defending An Loc. So effective were these air strikes that by late June the NVA forces attacking An Loc had lost all of their armor and artillery.

AC-119 and AC-130 gunships proved especially effective as 'tank busters' in the Central Highlands and Northern Provinces. B-52s got their share of tanks, too. In April, for example, six B-52s knocked out 35 NVA tanks during a saturation raid near Quang Tri. Strike aircraft were re-deployed to South Vietnam and Thailand during the invasion to help stop the Communist thrust, and by the summer the NVA had been forced to withdraw from much of the captured territory, but NVA units remained in control of substantial parts of South Vietnam.

During the 'Easter Invasion' sorties over North and South Vietnam combined averaged 15,000 per month. Also, beginning in May, air

strikes against the North were again authorized. In retaliation for the invasion of the South, most of the old limitations on targets were taken off in this new air offensive against the North which was nicknamed 'Linebacker'. In addition to mining Haiphong and other harbors for the first time, bridges, rail lines, fuel dumps, power plants, SAM sites, and AA batteries were all hit hard. All sorts of ECM (Electronic Countermeasures) aircraft were committed against North Vietnamese air defenses to minimize U.S. losses.

In response to the heavy U.S. attacks, the MiGs began coming back up, especially in the Hanoi/Haiphong area. As a result, all three USAF Vietnam aces recorded their fifth kills in the period August–October, 1972. Capt. Richard S. Ritchie, an F-4C pilot, got his fifth MiG on 28 August. Capt. Charles DeBellevue, who had been Ritchie's weapons systems officer, became the second ace on 9 September when he destroyed his fifth and sixth MiGs. And, another weapons systems officer, Capt. Jeffrey Feinstein, became the third USAF ace on 13 October.

Opposite:
B-52 pilot, showing helmet and oxygen gear used by jet pilots in Vietnam. Note squadron insignia on the left breast.

Above:
Air Force Pararescueman dons SCUBA gear in preparation for a rescue at sea. Note the flying suits on other crewmen.

Operations above the 20th Parallel were halted again on 23 October as peace negotiations were resumed, but when the North Vietnamese walked out of the talks on 13 December, the President ordered the raids to begin once again. 'Linebacker II' commenced on 18 December against previously restricted targets in the Hanoi/Haiphong area. F-105s, F-4s, F-111s, and B-52s all took part in the strikes, which were primarily at night, since to avoid the 'Wild Weasels' the NVA SAMs were optically controlled. During the 11 days the attacks lasted, the North Vietnamese launched their entire inventory of SAMs, almost a thousand of them. As a result, during the last two days of 'Linebacker II' the B-52s flew over Hanoi unmolested.

'Linebacker II' hit North Vietnam harder than any previous air strikes, and on 30 December, the North Vietnamese agreed to begin negotiating again, and air attacks were once again restricted to below the 20th Parallel. On 28 January 1973, the cease-fire went into effect, and U.S. combat missions ended. 'Peace with honor' was about to begin. Except for some advisory missions, remaining USAF personnel left South Vietnam during the first months of 1973, though many strike units remained based in Thailand.

During its commitment in Vietnam the USAF had lost 2257 aircraft and 2118 personnel KIA. There were 586 Air Force Prisoners of War or Missing of which 368 were returned. Well over six million tons of ordnance were dispersed by the USAF in Southeast Asia, more than twice that used in World War II and Korea combined. Twelve members of the USAF won Congressional Medals of Honor in Vietnam. Statistics, however, are not sufficient to summarize the importance of the USAF in the Vietnam War. Beyond a doubt, U.S. air power was the single most important factor in keeping the Communists at bay, and it was only after this steel umbrella had been removed from the combat zone that the Communists were able to achieve their victory.

Air Rescue and Recovery

One of the least heralded but most important Air Force units in Southeast Asia was the Aerospace Rescue and Recovery Service which carried out rescues of American and allied airmen downed over enemy territory. One group of men assigned to the ARRS were also probably the least well-known 'elite' unit in Vietnam. These were the Pararescuemen, or as they were known in Air

AC-47 pilot wearing many of the uniform items unique to the USAF in Vietnam. He wears the blue sidecap with his flight suit, mesh survival vest and .38 Special revolver. An M16 makes good insurance in case he is shot down.

Force jargon – the PJs. Trained as medics, paratroopers, frogmen, and rangers, the PJs were the ones who went down to administer first aid or help injured crewmen board the rescue chopper. Often, these rescue missions were carried out under hostile fire. There were probably never more than 125 PJs in Southeast Asia at any one time, but they rescued many times their number of downed pilots.

The first six members of the ARRS arrived in Vietnam in April, 1962. Their earliest rescues were carried out using borrowed Army or Marine Corps helicopters which were not designed for rescue missions.

Even with improper equipment, the ARRS carried out many rescues in 1963 and 1964.

Finally, in May, 1965, a more suitable chopper, the HH-3E 'Jolly Green Giant' was assigned to the ARRS. The ARRS was also operating HU-16 amphibious aircraft out of Da Nang to rescue pilots down in the Gulf of Tonkin. By June, 1965, ARRS choppers were operating out of Bien Hoa, Da Nang, Udorn, Nakhon Phanom, Takhli, and Korat.

For rescues over hostile territory, where most of them were carried out, the ARRS developed the SARTAF technique in which two choppers – one high and one low – carried out the rescue while A-1E Skyraiders flew cover to 'neutralize' any enemy force approaching the downed aircrewmen. The low chopper went in for the rescue, while the high one stood by in case it was downed or needed assistance.

Both the 'Jolly Green' and 'Super Jolly' were fitted with 'jungle penetrators'. These penetrators were attached to a winch and cable and were fitted with three fold down paddle seats. The penetrator was designed to crash through the thick canopy over much of Southeast Asia. Once it was lowered, downed aircrewmen would normally be hoisted into the chopper aboard it. If the pilot or crewman was injured, however, a PJ would ride the penetrator down to assist him or give emergency medical treatment.

In June, 1966, the 3rd Aerospace Rescue and Recovery Group was activated at Tan Son Nhut and given responsibility for rescues throughout Southeast Asia. Its command post – the Joint Search and Rescue Center – was also at Tan Son Nhut. The 3rd ARRG controlled four squadrons – the 37th at Da Nang, the 38th at Tan Son Nhut, the 39th at Tuy Hoa, and the 40th at Udorn.

The more sorties U.S. airmen flew, the more business the ARRS had. Because of the high pitch of air operations during 1968, that was the peak year for rescues, 916 men being picked up by the ARRS. By 1973, the ARRS had saved 3883 downed pilots and aircrewmen in Southeast Asia. In the process, they had lost 71 rescuemen and 45 aircraft.

Originally, defense of USAF installations in the Republic of Vietnam was handled by ARVN units, but after attacks on air bases such as the one in November, 1964, on Bien Hoa, it became obvious that increased security was going to be necessary. As a result, Air Police (later called Security Police, by which name they will be referred to from now on) units were deployed to Vietnam for security duties. By 1965, SPs and Air Force sentry dogs were in Vietnam protect-

Pararescueman fires the mini-gun from a Super Jolly Green Giant. Note flight helmet, special flight suit, flak jacket, survival vest, jungle boots and equipment belt.

ing Air Force installations and personnel.

The SPs developed a three zone defensive system on U.S. air bases. The exterior zone was composed of mines, lights, barriers, and intruder alarms with observation posts at key points. The second zone consisted of bunkers manned by SPs with M60 GPMGs and patrolling sentry dogs and their handlers. Teams were on alert to reinforce the bunkers or dog teams immediately if enemy contact were made. The interior zone was designed to protect the critical areas of the base (i.e. flight line, hangers, aircraft, barracks, etc.). More bunkers, lights, and sentry dog patrols covered the interior. Quick reaction teams manned jeeps mounted with M60s to reinforce other areas or protect this interior zone. Theoretically, attackers would be identified in

Air Force Pararescueman being awarded the AFC wears the tan 1505 uniform. Senior parachutists wings and aircrewmans wings are both worn. Although the three stripes worn indicate a buck sergeant prior to 1968 three stripes indicated Airman 1st Class, two an Airman 2nd Class and one an Airman 3rd Class. A3C was eliminated around 1968, after which time three stripes indicated sergeants rank.

the exterior zone and 'neutralized' in the middle zone. SPs were trained to react aggressively to intruders, and taking prisoners was not considered a high priority. In practice, this system worked relatively well until the Tet Offensive in early 1968 when the mass attacks on Bien Hoa and Tan Son Nhut proved it to be too static.

By 1968, Security Police squadrons were assigned to each of the major air bases used by the USAF in Vietnam: Da Nang, Pleiku, Nha Trang, Bien Hoa, Tan Son Nhut, Binh Thuy, Phu Cat, Tuy Hoa, Cam Ranh Bay, and Phan Rang. SP Squadrons were also assigned to major bases in

Thailand, especially Nakhon Phanom where much classified activity was going on. Each SP squadron was divided into three flights. At first, one flight was assigned to each eight hour shift, but experience taught that a higher proportion of men was needed on duty during the 2000–0400 hours period so adjustments were made to put more men on duty at this time. Quick reaction alert teams normally had a strength of 13 men.

Throughout 1966 and 1967, attacks against air bases were relatively frequent, but Tet marked the high tide of attacks against U.S. bases. During the attacks at Bien Hoa and Tan Son Nhut, more than 2000 VC were killed before the bases were secured.

It took the massive Tet attacks to convince the Air Force that it needed more highly trained units capable of handling mass attacks or infiltrations. During early 1967, 200 men selected from the top 10 per cent. of the Air Force's SPs had been assigned to the 1041st Security Police

AC-123 'Ranch Hand' defoliation pilots illustrate the rather diverse choice of equipment among some flying personnel. Both wear flak jackets, but the man at left also wears a survival vest and the flak shorts which were rarely seen. The pilots seem fond of World War II German gear. The man at left holds an MP10 SMG, the figure at right carries a Hitler Youth Knife.

Squadron as part of 'Operation Safeside'. These men had received 16 weeks of rigorous training similar to that of the Army's Rangers at Schofield Barracks, Hawaii. Upon completion of training the 1041st was assigned to Vietnam for six months where their training and motivation proved far superior for base defense than the normal SP squadron.

As a result, special Air Force units known as Combat Security Police Squadrons were formed and trained in a manner which combined the best elements of the U.S. Army Ranger school and the training of the British RAF Regiment. In addition to receiving more intensive training than normal SP squadrons, the CSP squadrons were organized more effectively to fight as light infantry. The establishment for a Combat Security Police Squadron called for 21 officers and 538 enlisted men. The squadron was broken into three flights, each with a strength of 6 officers and 161 enlisted men. Three field sections consisting of one officer and 32 enlisted men and one support section of one officer and 63 enlisted men made up a flight. The section was broken into ten man fire elements, which were divided into two man fire teams. The support section contained sentry dog teams (including some animals trained as scout dogs to give silent warning of the enemy when on ambushes), a surveillance element equipped with radar and other detection gear, and a weapons element armed with 81 mm. mortars, .50 caliber MGs, 7.62 mm. mini-guns, and grenade launchers. This organization granted the CSP squadron great flexibility in dealing with enemy attacks.

Three CSP squadrons – 821, 822, and 823 – were formed, with the 821st being deployed to Vietnam in April, 1968, to be followed by the other units in rotation. One CSP squadron would be serving in Vietnam until February, 1971. Although theoretically assigned to Phan Rang, flights or sections of the CSP squadron were often sent elsewhere on special assignment.

The four-footed SPs were also extremely important in defending air bases in Vietnam and Thailand. Sentry dogs 'alerted' time and time again preventing enemy infiltrators from penetrating a base's defenses. Sentry dogs even found intruders completely submerged in water, and dogs such as 'Nemo', a sentry dog at Tan Son Nhut who killed two VC despite a severe head wound, drove home their attacks even in the face of enemy fire. Dogs also saved their handlers many times from deadly kraits, often taking the snake bites themselves.

Even after U.S. troops had been withdrawn from Vietnam, the SPs mission was not complete. Not only did SPs continue to provide security at bases in Thailand, but SPs were sent back into Saigon from Clark AFB, Philippines, to provide security for the remaining Americans during the evacuation before the fall of Saigon.

Uniforms and Equipment

Many airmen assigned to Southeast Asia wore uniforms very similar to those worn by their counterparts in the States. Most commonly worn

LTC Joe Jackson, USAF receives the Congressional Medal of Honor from President Johnson. In addition to a side view of Jackson's 'blues', this offers a good view of USN and USMC dress uniforms on the other award recipients.

headgear was probably the baseball style green utility cap, though certain airmen wore caps of other colors to indicate special assignments. Some groundcrewmen, for example, wore red ones. Also widely worn was the blue garrison cap. Officers wore their insignia pinned to the left side of this cap. Also worn, on occasion, was the blue service cap with either officers or enlisted mens cap insignia attached. Special personnel had distinctive headgear of their own. The Air Commandos wore their own hat which was a type of bush hat with one or both sides turned up. Rank insignia was pinned to the front. Many pilots in both Vietnam and Thailand affected this hat also. Berets were worn by Air Force 'elite' personnel. The Pararescuemen wore a maroon beret with the pararescue badge bearing the motto 'That Others May Live'. Combat Controllers who operated behind enemy lines to call in air strikes wore a dark blue beret with airborne

wings as a beret badge. Originally, the only Security Policemen authorized to wear berets were the Combat Security Police who wore a blue one. Eventually, however, all SPs were authorized to wear the blue beret. SPs also wore Army style 'boonie' camouflage hats or steel helmets with camo covers. When flying, of course, most pilots wore one of the various Air Force flying helmets. Jet pilots were equipped with oxygen masks, etc., while helicopter or light fixed wing pilots wore a lighter helmet similar to that worn by Army aviators.

Basic USAF uniform in Southeast Asia was green utilities worn with blue U.S. AIR FORCE and name tapes. Frequently on this or other uniforms a unit patch would be worn on the right pocket. Also widely worn was the short sleeved tan '1505' uniform which was authorized for wear year round in Southeast Asia. Generally speaking, anyone engaged in relatively strenuous activity wore the utilities, while anyone with an office job wore 1505s. Also occasionally worn were 'blues' consisting of dark blue tunic, trousers, and tie, and light blue shirt. This was the standard Air Force dress uniform, but because of the climate was not normally worn in Southeast Asia. Later in the war, an informal blue uniform consisting of short sleeved blue shirt and dark blue trousers came into use and was worn in Vietnam.

Air Force special units wore uniforms similar to those in use by other elite units. Combat controllers, PJs, and SPs all wore camouflage utilities – tiger stripes in the earlier stages of the war and leaf pattern later. Members of these three units were normally the only Air Force personnel authorized to blouse their trousers. It took the intervention of the 7th Air Force flight surgeon, however, to allow troops to roll their utility sleeves above the elbow. Pilots normally wore NOMEX flying suits or in the case of jet pilots pressurized suits, though chopper or transport pilots sometimes flew in standard utilities. PJs, helicopter door gunners, or SPs frequently wore flak jackets similar the Army.

Black combat boots were standard Air Force issue, though many airmen, especially Combat Controllers, PJs, and SPs, were issued jungle boots. Chukka boots which came just above the ankles were issued to some enlisted personnel and were sometimes worn in Southeast Asia by groundcrewmen or other technical ratings. With 1505s and 'blues', black 'low quarter' dress shoes were normally worn.

Normally the only Air Force personnel who wore webbed gear were the Combat Controllers and the Security Police. Since they operated in enemy territory, Combat Controllers were usually equipped much as were the Army's LRRPs or Special Forces with pistol belt and suspenders and lightweight or tropical rucksack. Combat Controllers had to hump the additional weight of a radio so they scrimped wherever possible on gear. Security Policemen normally wore the pistol belt and load bearing suspenders, though often a distinctive Air Force magazine pouch made of nylon and holding two M16 magazines was used instead of the standard Army issue ones. Army pouches were, however, issued to some units as well. Additionally, on the belt or suspenders SPs wore a two-way radio, flashlight, poncho, survival/fighting knife (usually the Jet Pilots Knife, but Randalls or Gerbers were also popular) or a bayonet, canteen, and first aid kit. In most cases, a revolver holster was also worn. Most SPs carried a package of 'C-rats' as well. Combat Security Policemen normally carried similar equipment, though if on an extended patrol a rucksack, entrenching tool, and rappelling rope might be added.

F-4E pilot returning his equipment after a mission; note the flight suits and helmets worn by Air Force fighter pilots during the Vietnam War.

Flight crews and Pararescuemen normally wore a pistol belt with revolver holster and knife attached. Many, however, also wore the Air Force's well-designed survival vest which contained everything from fire starting aids and compass to an arrowhead for hunting. Some vests had a holster for a revolver and a sheath for a knife built in. Once again, the most popular knife was the Jet Pilot's knife.

Air Force sentry dogs were issued their own equipment, consisting of collars, leashes, chains, muzzles, feeding dishes, combs, brushes, etc. Dog handlers would often be festooned with gear for the dog and perhaps an extra canteen of water for the 'pooch'. An interesting note on the high regard the SPs felt for their dogs is that many 're-upped' or extended for a second tour in Vietnam rather than leave the dog they had walked 'PMs' (perimeter guards) with for a year. The author remembers a rumor when he was in OTS (Air Force Officers Training School) that anyone washing out of OTS was sent directly to Vietnam as a dog handler. An ex-SP sergeant when asked about this rumor replied, 'Certainly not. We think too much of the dogs to do that to them.'

Except for the Special Forces, no U.S. unit in Vietnam had the wealth of insignia of the Air Force. Air Force squadrons have always had colorful pocket or jacket patches, and those serving in Vietnam or Thailand were no exception. As with the Special Forces, many Air Force insignia were locally produced in limited numbers and as a result are quite rare. Many patches were the usual fanciful ones associated with fighter or bomber squadrons. One for a 'Wild Weasel' unit, for example, bears a flying weasel about to throw a missile at a target, while others bore the usual run of cartoon characters. More standard patches bore the crests of Air Force commands such as the Strategic Air Command or the Aerospace Rescue and Recovery Service.

Pilots and aircrewmen wore their wings on the left breast, in silver on 1505s or blues and in

USAF flight surgeon Capt. James Graham Jr served in his medical capacity and flew combat missions over North Vietnam with the 8th TFW. The equipment U.S. Air Force pilots wore in the cockpit is well shown. Note the S & W .38 Special revolver strapped to his hip.

subdued cloth on their utilities or flight suits. PJs and Combat Controllers wore their parachutists wings on the left breast, once again in silver with 1505s or blues and in subdued cloth on utilities or flight suits. PJs wore both aircrew and parachutists wings. Air Policemen or Security Policemen wore their badges on the left breast, and though

badges were not always worn on them, both silver and cloth versions were used on utilities.

By far the most ubiquitous weapon among USAF personnel was the .38 Special Smith & Wesson revolver with a 4 inch barrel. This weapon was issued to aircrewmen, SPs, Combat Controllers, and PJs as a matter of course. Others who might have need for a weapon were also often issued the .38 Special. In certain situations, 2 inch barreled revolvers were available for undercover work, but only Office of Special Investigations (OSI) personnel were normally issued these weapons.

Although the M1 and M2 carbines were issued to SPs very early in the war, the M16 was adopted by the Air Force (as the AR15) even before the Army. Normally, regular SPs were issued the M16, while dog handlers were issued the shorter CAR15. Combat Controllers, PJs and CSPs also preferred the CAR15. Many pilots, especially those assigned to Air Commando units, also tucked an M16 or some other full auto weapon into their planes in case they were shot down.

The only Air Force units assigned heavier weapons were the SPs and CSPs. Normally available were the M60 GPMG, the M79 grenade launcher, the M203 M16 mounted 40 mm. grenade launcher, and Stevens or Remington 12 gauge riot shotguns. Heavier weapons available to the CSP squadrons included the XM174 rapid fire 40 mm. grenade launcher with 12 round magazine, the M67 90 mm. recoilless rifle, M29 81 mm. mortar, M72 LAW, M20 .50 caliber MG, and the GAU-2B/A 7.62 mm. mini-gun. The usual range of grenades – the M26A1, M18 smoke, and M34 'Willie Pete' – were also carried by the SPs and CSPs.

Though not part of the Air Force, one other group of aviators should be mentioned. Air America was a 'commercial' airline funded by the CIA which flew missions all over Southeast Asia. These included everything from insertion of agents to 'hard rice' (arms, etc.) drops. Air America pilots wore just about whatever type of flight suit they pleased, though a grey uniform roughly similar to that of commercial airline pilots was somewhat standardized.

7 Republic of Vietnam Armed Forces

The Vietnamese Army

Although many Vietnamese served with the French Union Forces, the Vietnamese Army was not created until 1949. After the Geneva Accords of July, 1954, an independent Army of the Republic of Vietnam became a necessity. This army, which began to take shape during 1955 and 1956, was geared to serve two purposes: an internal security force and a deterrent to the Communists in the north. One of the earliest problems was developing a logistics system since even after 1954, the Vietnamese had continued to rely on French supply channels.

As of the Geneva Accords in 1954, the South Vietnamese Army consisted of 152 infantry battalions, 2 airborne battalions, 2 imperial guard battalions, 2 highland infantry battalions, 2 armored cavalry squadrons, 6 artillery battalions, and 5 engineer battalions. During 1955 these forces were reorganized into 4 field divisions each with a strength of 8100 troops, 6 light divisions each with a strength of 5800 troops, and miscellaneous territorial regiments.

Reorganization of the Vietnamese forces continued, however, in an attempt to field an effective fighting force. By September, 1959, ARVN forces consisted of 7 divisions, each with a strength of 10,450 men. Each division was organized into three infantry regiments, an artillery battalion, a mortar battalion, an engineer battalion, and company sized support units. In addition there were 5 airborne battalions and 4 armored cavalry regiments equipped with M-24 light tanks and M-8 self-propelled howitzers. Almost 90,000 members of the Civil Guard and Self-Defense Corps, which were provincial or local forces assigned to internal security duties, supplemented the regular army.

By 1959 service schools had been established to train men for the Vietnamese Army as follows: National Military Academy at Dalat; National NCO Academy at Nha Trang; Command and General Staff College and Medical, Military Intelligence, and Language Schools at Saigon; Infantry, Artillery, Armor, and Signal Schools, Administrative Schools (Quartermaster, etc.)

ARVN tabs. First: Ranger. Second: Ranger. Third: 81st Battalion, LLDB, Recon Force. Bottom: LRRP.

and Ordnance School at Thu Duc; Transportation School at Quang Trung; Engineer School at Vung Tau; Military Police School at Da Nang. Other highly specialized schools such as the Commando Training School at Nha Trang where the nucleus of the Vietnamese Special Forces were trained existed as well. Many ARVN troops were also given special training in the U.S.A.

By 1959 the Viet Cong were looming as a larger threat than an invasion from the North, and it became obvious that South Vietnamese troops would have to be organized and trained to fight a counterinsurgency war, while still retaining the capability of stopping a full-scale invasion.

By 1960 in an attempt to stem the growing tide of Viet Cong successes, Ranger companies had been created in each infantry battalion. The Vietnamese Special Forces – the Luc Luong Duc Biet – had also been created as a counterinsurgency force. By 1960 there were about 9000 ARVN Rangers, though their standards of training were still little better than that of regular infantry. By 1961, however, U.S. Special Forces and Rangers had established a Ranger School at Duc My (other Rangers were trained at Trung Lap and Tet Son) and there were soon 86 well-trained Ranger companies available for counter-insurgency duties. As the war progressed, the ARVN Rangers (the Biet-Dong-Quan) became the units most feared by the VC. At one point there was even a hit song about the BDQs, the Vietnamese equivalent of the 'Ballad of the Green Berets'. The ARVN green berets – the LLDB – numbered 600 by 1961 and were used as LRRPs and as co-advisors with the U.S. Special Forces in training local civilian irregulars. Also by 1961 ARVN intelligence forces had been increased to aid in analyzing data so that the enemy could be effectively countered. During 1961 the training of Rangers, Civil Guards, and the Self-Defense Corps was given top priority.

By August of 1963 the South Vietnamese regular army totaled 192,000 troops organized into 4 corps, 9 divisions, 1 airborne brigade, 1 Special Forces Group, 3 separate regiments, 1 territorial regiment, 86 Ranger companies, and 19 separate battalions. Through 1963 and 1964 the Regional Forces and Popular Forces, as the Civil Guard and Self-Defense Corps were now known, continued to increase in strength as well.

During 1965 as American troops began to arrive in Vietnam in large numbers, the South Vietnamese Army was also expanded from 119 battalions to 149 battalions, including 2 more airborne battalions. Regional and Popular Forces strength was increased to over 300,000 at the same time. Ranger companies had also been reorganized into battalions to cope with larger NVA and Main Force VC units.

Actual ARVN strength increased little in 1966, but improvements were made in replacement and training procedures, in command and control, and in psy ops capability. ARVN units also began to take part in major offensive operations with American and other allied troops. At the end of 1966, authorized ARVN strength stood at 277, 363 regulars. In addition there were 141,731 in the Regional Forces and 176,254 in the Popular Forces. However, through desertions, casualties, etc. actual strengths were sometimes as much as 10 per cent. below those given.

During 1967 a freeze was put on increases in the South Vietnamese Army. ARVN units continued to be involved in major operations during that year including 'Cedar Falls' and 'Enterprise' (which included 'Ruff Puffs' as well as ARVN regulars). Both of these operations took place early in the year, however, and as 1967 progressed ARVN units were used more frequently as security units to aid pacification of the countryside, while more heavily armed U.S. troops carried out the search and destroy missions. It can be justly argued that this policy was a bad one since it hindered the development of ARVN combat ability and also caused hard feelings among U.S. troops who saw ARVN units assigned to 'safe' missions, while the 'grunts' took casualties. The Biet-Dong-Quan (ARVN Rangers), now organized into groups instead of battalions, continued to see more than their share of combat as did some of the Special Forces trained 'indigs'.

REPUBLIC OF VIETNAM FORCES

Marine This figure wears the older style tiger stripes and steel helmet with camo cover. The shoulder sleeve insignia is that of the Marine Brigade. The older style canteen with chained lid is carried as it was by the U.S. Marines. His weapon is the M60 GPMG. **Air Marshal Nguyen Cao Ky** Marshal Ky's black flight suit and bright scarves gave him a dashing air. On his right breast is the insignia of the 518th A-1 Skyraider Squadron, while on his left breast is that of the 83rd Special Group. His weapon is a U.S. .45 automatic carried on a much worn GI issue pistol belt.
Junk Force Sailor This sailor's black beret with the junk force badge identifies his assignment. He wears only black 'pajama' trousers and beret. His tattoo 'SAT CONG', means 'Kill Communists'.

REPUBLIC OF VIETNAM

Marine

Air Marshal Nguyen Cao Ky

Junk Force Sailor

Very smart Vietnamese paratroopers serving with the French. Note the jaunty angle the maroon beret is worn at, ribbons on left breast, parachutists brevet on the right breast and fourragères to designate unit award for gallantry.

Upper left: ARVN airborne wings. Upper right: LLDB airborne wings. Lower: Thai airborne wings.

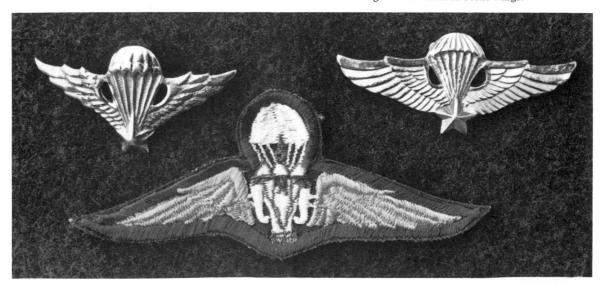

After the Tet Offensive in 1968 the South Vietnamese Army had a greater sense of confidence and purpose. Many Viet units fought with particular courage and determination during Tet. Ranger and airborne units, for example, helped secure Saigon in Operation 'Tran Hung Dao'. More than 80,000 conscripts were taken into the armed forces in 1968, most going to the Army. As a result of the Tet Offensive and the beginnings of Vietnamization, ARVN units began to assume more responsibility for offensive operations.

Reflecting its increased responsibility, the Army grew to a strength of 341,869 in 1968. Regional Force strength stood at 211,932 and Popular Force strength stood at 179,015. Further increases in 1969 and 1970 were intended to raise Army strength to 355,135 and Regional Force strength to 218,687.

During 1970, of course, the most important ARVN operation was the move into Cambodia commanded by Lt Gen. Do Cao Tri, one of the best of the South Vietnamese generals.

By 1970 ARVN training facilities had been greatly increased and had grown more sophisticated as well, enabling the increasing manpower to be trained. As of 1970 the only personnel still being trained outside of Vietnam were pilots and some communications specialists.

The major operation of 1971, though, was 'Lam Son 719' during which ARVN forces moved into Laos in an attempt to cut the Ho Chi Minh Trail. This operation had U.S. air support, but U.S. ground troops were not involved. At best 'Lam Son 719' was probably a draw.

On 30 March 1972 the Communists began their massive Easter Offensive. Initially, three ARVN divisions, two Marine brigades, and the Military Region I (formerly I Corps) Ruff Puffs were all that blocked the Communist forces advancing from the north and west. The ARVN 1st Division resisted strongly at some fire support bases and other strongpoints, but by the end of

Republic of Vietnam Police Chief (left) wearing green utilities and carrying an S & W revolver tucked into his belt, and interpreter (center) wearing flop hat and 'pajamas', with an USMC officer. All three carry M1 Carbines.

April most of these positions had been captured. Elements of the 1st Division along with Marines and an airborne brigade defended Hue, and by 15 May the 1st Division had re-occupied many of the positions lost at the end of April.

In April Communist forces had also struck towards Saigon from Cambodia. The critical blocking point proved to be An Loc, and the South Vietnamese prepared to defend it. ARVN Rangers were among the defenders of An Loc, and the 21st ARVN Division and an airborne brigade from the General Reserve were sent as reinforcements. By 18 June the siege of An Loc had been lifted.

One other Communist attack from the west took place in II Corps where the Communist thrust from Cambodia towards Kontum City which was well defended by Rangers and airborne forces. Although fighting was fierce, by 31 May the Communists were retreating.

South Vietnamese forces – especially the Rangers, Marines, airborne units, and the 1st Divison – had fought relatively well during the Easter Offensive, though they had still relied heavily on U.S. air support to turn the tide.

By December, 1972, when the U.S. Army had almost completely pulled out, ARVN strength stood as follows:

I Corps
    1st, 2nd, 3rd Infantry Divisions
    1st Ranger Group
    1st Armored Brigade
    Airborne Division
II Corps
    22nd, 23rd Infantry Divisions
    2nd Ranger Group
    2nd Armored Brigade
III Corps
    5th, 18th, 25th Infantry Divisions
    3rd, 5th, 6th, 81st Ranger Groups
    3rd Armored Brigade
IV Corps
    7th 9th, 21st Infantry Divisions
    4th Ranger Group
    4th Armored Brigade
    41st, 42nd Border Ranger Group (formerly CIDG)

Throughout 1973 and 1974 North Vietnamese strength increased as the Communists continued to probe the South for weakness. The South Vietnamese armed forces, on the other hand, suffered from cuts in U.S. aid. On 10 March 1975 the Communists launched what was to be their final offensive. Despite far superior total numbers of South Vietnamese troops, the North Vietnamese rolled up easy victories in the northern provinces, and the South Vietnamese decided to evacuate the highlands, precipitating a rout. Over 100,000 South Vietnamese troops were taken prisoner, while many thousands more discarded their weapons and equipment and became a leaderless rabble. Without U.S. airpower or advisors the Army of the Republic of Vietnam virtually collapsed. Morale was so low in the South Vietnamese armed forces and corruption so rampant that only a token resistance was made. There were a few exceptions. Some Rangers, paratroopers, and LLDBs fought well; a few of these 'elite' troops along with former members of the National Police also took to the 'bush' after the capitulation of South Vietnam on 30 April. From that date the Republic of Vietnam ceased to exist as did its armed forces.

Uniforms and Equipment

No other military force in Vietnam wore the diversity of headgear that was worn by the Army of the Republic of Vietnam and the Regional and Popular Forces. The standard ARVN enlisted headgear was a khaki beret with a beret badge bearing a sword and triangle superimposed over a circle. Officers wore a service hat with a cap badge bearing the South Vietnamese coat of arms. After 1968 enlisted personnel in non special units began wearing a service cap instead of the beret for walking out.

Special and elite units also wore berets. Para-

REPUBLIC OF VIETNAM, ARVN
ARVN Ranger Officer This captain wears the tropical khaki uniform with maroon beret bearing bullion BDQ (Biet Dong Quan) badge. He wears the Ranger patch on his sleeve, rank insignia on both collars, the Ranger badge and Vietnamese parachutists wings, on his right breast, and U.S. parachutists wings on the left breast along with ribbons for service and valor. **ARNV Paratrooper, Circa 1960** Equipped, for the most part, with U.S. World War II era equipment, this para wears green utilities with black combat boots, and M-1 steel helmet with netting, and U.S. webbed gear, including a bandolier of M-1 Garand clips, along with a bayonet for the M-1 rifle which he carries. **LLDB (Vietnamese Special Forces) Trooper** This LLDB wears one of the spotted patterns of camo issued through the U.S. Special Forces. He has Vietnamese jump wings on his right breast and U.S. jump wings on his left breast, Vietnamese Special Forces shoulder sleeve insignia, and, on his green beret, the later pattern LLDB beret badge. A U.S. M1A1 paratrooper's carbine with stock folded and .45 automatic pistol comprise his armament.

REPUBLIC OF VIETNAM

ARVN Ranger Officer

LLDB
(Vietnamese Special Forces)
Trooper

ARVN Paratrooper, Circa 1960

troopers wore red berets with a winged parachute beret badge. Rangers wore a maroon beret with a winged arrow superimposed on a wreath beret badge. The LLDB wore a green beret with a beret badge bearing a five pointed star, a sword, and a parachute superimposed on an annulet. Later in the war this beret badge was replaced by one similar to that of the airborne forces. The Provincial Reconnaissance Units (PRUs), elite airborne qualified personnel often assigned to the Phoenix Program, wore various colours of beret depending upon their province and advisors. Black, red, green and camo berets were all worn by PRUs, often with the winged scimitar beret badge. The special 'Hac Bao' (Black Panther) strike company of the 1st Division also wore black berets with a beret badge depicting a black panther superimposed on an annulet.

Rangers, LLDBs, Ruff Puffs, PRUs, etc. at times also wore camouflage berets and camo or OD boonie hats. Ruff Puffs, especially early in the war, often wore the floppy tan French style jungle hat, too.

The basic ARVN helmet was the same as the U.S. helmet, while ARVN Rangers and paras normally wore the M-1 parachutist's helmet. Often these helmets were either painted in camo colors or were fitted with camouflage covers. The Rangers normally had their distinctive – and feared – panther's head on five pointed star insignia on their helmet or camo cover as well. South Vietnamese armored crewmen wore specialized U.S. helmets.

Standard ARVN uniform for enlisted personnel was a khaki shirt with khaki trousers. A khaki tie was also sometimes worn. Chevrons were worn on the left upper arm. Officers wore a khaki tunic over a khaki shirt and tie with khaki trousers. Black shoulder boards bearing rank insignia were worn on the tunic. Unit insignia were sometimes worn on the upper shirt or tunic arm as well.

Green utilities similar to those issued to American troops were the standard combat uniform. Rangers, LLDB, PRUs, paratroopers, National Police Field Force, or other special troops normally wore tiger stripes, leaf pattern, or some type of locally produced camouflage pattern. Unit insignia was normally worn on the upper arm, though occasionally it was worn on the pocket. Ruff Puff insignia was normally worn on the pocket. In some cases insignia might be worn on either or both shoulders and the pocket or any combination thereof. Airborne wings,

Ranger badges, or other qualification badges might also be worn on the breast. Ruff Puffs in the early days often wore a tan or light brown utility uniform of French style, but later wore green utilities.

ARVN Rangers, LLDB paratroopers, Ruff Puffs, and some other units wore silk scarves of different colors. These colors – most often red, yellow, blue, or green – were used to distinguish different companies. Flak jackets were not as commonly used by ARVN troops as by U.S. troops, but some were worn. In many cases they were given to the ARVNs when U.S. troops were issued newer ones. Their bulk and weight, however, made them uncomfortable for the smaller ARVNs to wear.

With the tan walking out uniform black low quarter shoes were the norm for conventional troops, while Rangers, paras, etc. wore jump boots with trousers bloused. Black combat boots were standard for field use, though Rangers, LLDBs, etc. wore American style jungle boots as soon as they were available. Eventually, other ARVN units received jungle boots as well.

ARVN troops normally used American webbed gear and magazine pouches. The American manufactured tropical rucksack with three pockets was issued to ARVN forces by the late 1960s, though some special units were issued indigenous rucks. Typically, many grenades would be hung from the webbed gear since ARVN troops were especially fond of grenades.

Few armies in history have had the wealth of insignia of the Army of the Republic of Vietnam. More than a thousand shoulder patches, tabs, distinctive insignia, and badges were worn by ARVN troops, and many of these were extremely colorful. Some insignia were beautifully embroidered on silk, while others were printed on cloth. Normally, divisional insignia was worn on the left sleeve, and sub unit insignia on the pockets. Qualification badges and beret badges were made in metal, bullion, and subdued or non-subdued cloth variations. Among the more commonly seen qualification badges were the Ranger badge consisting of crossed swords over a wreath with a star above; the Reconnaissance Qualified badge consisting of winged hands holding binoculars; and parachutists wings consisting of a winged parachute with a star below. Regular para wings and Special Forces wings differed slightly. Both, however, were available in basic, senior, and master configurations. Viet qualification badges were normally worn on the right

USMC officer inspects Republic of Vietnam Popular
Forces troops.

breast. Airborne qualified personnel usually
wore U.S. jump wings on their left breast.

Generals rank was indicated by one through
five stars as in the U.S. Army. Chuan Tuong (sub
or brigadier general) wore one star; Thieu Tuong
(junior or major general) wore two stars; Trung
Tuong (intermediate or lieutenant general) wore
three stars; Dai Tuong (senior general or general)
wore four stars; and Dai Tuong (superior general
or General of the Army) wore five stars. A Dai Ta
(colonel) wore three silver plum blossoms; a
Trung Ta (lieutenant colonel) two silver plum
blossoms; a Thieu Ta (major) one silver plum
blossom; a Dai Uy (captain) three gold plum
blossoms; a Trung Uy (first lieutenant) two gold
plum blossoms; and a Thieu Uy (second lieutenant) one gold plum blossom. Officer cadets or
aspirants wore a gold button with a raised
symbol. Warrant officers wore a plain gold button. Officers rank insignia on utilities or cammies
were often worn on the lapel about at the
breastbone.

Among NCOs, a master sergeant wore a single
gold button; a sergeant 1st class three silver
chevrons; a sergeant one silver chevron; a corporal first class one silver and two gold chevrons;
a corporal two gold chevrons, and a private first
class one gold chevron.

After 1968 captains, first lieutenants, and second lieutenants wore three, two, and one silver

plum blossoms respectively, while colonels,
lieutenant colonels, and majors wore the same
types of plum blossoms but over a bar. There
were also some changes in the NCO rank insignia
when master sergeants and master sergeants first
class began wearing their chevrons on black
epaulets.

Up until 1967 ARVN troops were armed with
a miscellany of older American weapons. The M1
and M2 carbines were most widely used, but M1
Garands, Thompson SMGs, and M3 'grease-
guns' all saw extensive service. Beginning with
airborne, Ranger, LLDB, and PRU units, the
M16 began to be issued to ARVN units in 1967.
By 1968 most ARVN regulars were armed with
M16s, M79s, M60s, and LAWs. As previously
mentioned, ARVN troops liked grenades and
used the older Mk 2 'pineapple' grenades as well
as M26A1s. The standard issue handgun for
ARVN troops was the Colt 1911A1 .45 auto,
though ARVN officers acquired S & W .38
Special revolvers whenever possible. Higher ranking officers were especially fond of the compact
J-frame, snub-nosed revolvers – one of which – a
Model 38 or 49 'Bodyguard' – was used by Police
Chief Nguyen Ngoc Loan to blow the brains out
of a Communist captured during the Tet
Offensive, an act recorded in one of the most
famous photographs of the war. Unfortunately,
the world press forgot to include the information
that the captured VC had just murdered the wife
and small children of one of Loan's co-officers in
especially brutal fashion.

The Vietnamese
Marine Corps

Premier Diem officially created the Vietnamese
Marine Corps in October, 1954. Most of the
original members were either former Army or
Navy commandos or former members of French
'dinassauts' (river assault divisions). Actually,
most of these transferees were elite assault troops
which gave the fledgling VNMC a strong basis to
build upon. By early 1955 approximately 2400
officers and men had been assigned to the
VNMC; many of them were organized into the
1st Landing Battalion at Nha Trang, the remainder were in company or smaller garrison units.

Because of cutbacks in naval strength, the
VNMC was reduced somewhat in strength dur-

Gen. Westmoreland and U.S. Sec. of Defense McNamara talk with Vietnamese officers. Westmoreland always wore his master parachutists badge on his hat above his four stars.

ing 1955, but it also got a chance to prove itself in combat against Hoa Hao dissidents in the Mekong Delta.

By early 1956 authorized VNMC strength had been set at 1837 men divided into two landing battalions each with a strength of 728 men, an HQ and service company, and a 4.2 inch mortar company.

VNMC strength remained stable for the next couple of years. The 1st Battalion, VNMC was based at Nha Trang, and the 2nd Battalion, VNMC was based at Cam Ranh Bay, though each battalion was also periodically rotated to a camp near Bien Hoa. At the end of 1958 the 1st VNMC Battalion began operating against VC guerrillas in An Xuyen Province. Conducting platoon and company sized operations in the swamps, the South Vietnamese Marines proved one of the most effective Vietnamese Armed Forces units.

During 1959 the 1st Battalion continued to operate in An Xuyen Province, while the 2nd Battalion began operating in Vinh Binh Province. Their successes helped convince the Diem government to increase the VNMC in mid-1959 to a strength of 2276 men through formation of the 3rd Landing Battalion. Most of the

strength for this new battalion came from amphibious units of the Army which were being phased out. Many officers and NCOs were also transferred from the other two battalions. The VNMC along with the ARVN Airborne Brigade were designated as the general reserve force for the Vietnamese Armed Forces.

1961 saw the VNMC expanded again to a strength of 3321. A fourth landing battalion was formed and a 75 mm. pack howitzer battery was added. Also in 1961 the Vietnamese Marines staged an amphibious assault against the VC on the Ca Mau Peninsula. But no VC were encountered, but it gave the VNMC experience at amphibious operations.

On 1 January 1962, the VNMC was expanded once again, this time into a brigade with a strength of 5483 troops. There were no new infantry battalions created, but an artillery battalion composed of one 105 mm. howitzer battery, two 75 mm. pack howitzer batteries, and an HQ and service battery was created. An amphibious support battalion was also formed which contained recon, communications, motor transport, medical, and engineering support troops. During 1962 elements of the brigade were involved in 23 combat operations which included 12 amphibious landings and eight chopper assaults.

During 1963 the normal pattern was for three VNMC battalions to be on combat operations while one battalion remained at Thu Duc as a quick reaction force.

In November the Vietnamese Marines took part in the coup which overthrew President Diem but were shortly back to fighting the enemy.

By 1964 the Vietnamese Marine Brigade had grown to a strength of 6109 men. During that year units of the VNMC saw action in the II, III, and IV corps tactical zones while still maintaining at least one battalion always in reserve. VNMC multi-battalion task forces were used extensively in the southernmost provinces. In July, 1964, the Marine Brigade was expanded

Republic of Vietnam, General Insignia
First row, left and right: 5th MIKE Force Command patch; 1st Bn VNMC patch; VNMC Bde shoulder sleeve insignia. *Second row:* 1st Infantry Div. Strike Coy; Vietnamese Ranger (Biet Dong Quan) shoulder insignia; Vietnamese Ranger beret badge in bullion. *Third row:* 1st Airborne Medical Coy; Vietnamese Airborne Div. shoulder sleeve insignia; 9th Parachute Bn 'beer can' insignia. *Fourth row:* Quang Ngai Province Provincial Recon Unit; Quang Nam Province PRU; 'Tony the Tiger' patch of the LLDB (Luc Luong Dac Biet – Vietnamese Special Forces).

U.S. trained Vietnamese Marine DI inspects Viet Marine recruits. The recruits wear both camouflage and green utilities. Note the DI's US style campaign hat.

Opposite above:
Men of the VNMC artillery with their USMC advisors. Note the VNMC dark green berets and camouflage utilities.

Opposite right:
USMC colonel inspects the M1 Garand of members of the VNMC at a rifle range near Saigon. The Garands were issued in an effort to increase VNMC marksmanship standards. Note beret badge of 2nd lieutenant (left foreground).

Opposite Far Right:
General Wallace M. Greene, Commandant of the Marine Corps (center) talking with a U.S. and Vietnamese officer. The U.S. officers wear the short-sleeved tropical khaki uniform, USMC insignia on the left of the sidecap and rank insignia on the right. Qualification badges were authorized for wear on this uniform and the LTC (right) wears parachutists wings. The Vietnamese officer wears a similar khaki uniform but with long sleeves and dark belt.

A USMC communications advisor with Vietnamese troops in the Rung Sat Special Zone. He wears camouflage, including his utility hat, and carries the .45 M3 SMG.

U.S. Naval advisor gives Vietnamese sailors instruction in use of the M16 rifle.

once again to a strength of 6555 by adding a fifth infantry battalion, though the new 5th Battalion was not fully combat ready until mid-1965. Also in 1964 the VNMC recruit center at Thu Duc became operational, meaning that Marines no longer had to train at ARVN recruit centers. On the last day of 1964, the 4th Vietnamese Battalion was hit very hard by Communist Main Force units numbering between 1000 and 2000 men from the 9th Viet Cong Division. This was the worst Vietnamese Marine defeat at that point in the war.

The VNMC at least partially avenged those losses in February, 1965, when they relieved the besieged town of Hoai An in Binh Dinh Province inflicting heavy VC casualties. Throughout 1965, in fact, the VNMC saw extensive combat both in independent actions and in conjunction with U.S. units. VNMC strength increased again in 1966 to 7172.

By 1968 the VNMC had increased only slight-ly to 7321 troops. Early in that year Vietnamese Marines were heavily involved in the fighting during the Tet Offensive.

As 'Vietnamization' began, the VNMC continued to increase in size in anticipation of taking over more and more responsibility for the war. The Vietnamese Marines were raised to divisional status by 1969 when their strength was nearly 11,000. The ARVN airborne forces had also been increased to divisional proportions and along with the Marine Division continued to provide the strategic reserve for the South Vietnamese armed forces during 1969 and 1970.

In 1971, however, the Marine Division was one of the formations chosen to take part in 'Lam Son 719' when one Marine brigade was assigned to act as the reserve in the vicinity of Khe Sanh.

In 1972 the Vietnamese Marines played an important role in recapturing lost ground after the Communist Easter offensive. The 258th Marine Brigade helped halt the enemy advance in the Dong Ha area, and Vietnamese Marines were instrumental in defending Hue. In September the marines recaptured Quang Tri City. During

the 1972 invasion the VNMC fought very well, showing that it justly deserved its elite status. As 1972 ended the Marine Division was in position near Quang Tri City. Marine strength at the time was divided among nine battalions assigned to the 147th, 258th, and 369th Marine Brigades.

In many ways the years after the American withdrawal found the VNMC returning to the role it had fulfilled in the early days of the counterinsurgency effort. Though now a division with a strength of 12–14,000 men, the VNMC still functioned primarily as a strategic reserve force deploying small units for patrolling or on COIN operations. Unrealistic use of the Marines in the defense of Da Nang when they were ordered to hastily withdraw from their positions near Hue resulted in their early elimination as an effective fighting force during the 1975 Communist invasion.

Uniforms and Equipment

Up until 1960 Vietnamese Marines wore a uniform which was basically a combination of the

Vietnamese infantrymen move through a rice paddy with their U.S. advisor. All wear uniforms typical of 1963–64.

Vietnamese Army and Navy uniforms. In 1960, however, in an attempt to instill esprit de corps in the VNMC a uniform consisting of a dark green beret and tiger striped camouflage utilities was adopted. A VNMC insignia consisting of an eagle, globe, and anchor similar to the USMC insignia but with a five pointed star and a map of Vietnam superimposed was also adopted at about this time for use as a beret badge and a shoulder sleeve insignia. The older insignia of the Marine infantry – a red star on a black circle – was also still occasionally used as well for a short while.

South Vietnamese Marines wore fatigue hats similar to those worn by U.S. Marines and U.S. style steel helmets with camouflage covers. By the mid-1960s VNMC drill instructors, many of whom had been trained in the U.S., wore USMC campaign or 'Smokey the Bear' hats.

Although the tiger striped camouflage utilities remained in general use with the VNMC, green utilities were also issued. A khaki walking out uniform similar to the USMC tropical khakis worn with a dark green belt was also in use by the mid-1960s. A dark green dickey and a fourragère were sometimes worn with the tiger striped uniform. Originally, black combat boots were standard with the tiger striped utilities but later jungle boots replaced them. Black dress shoes were standard with the khaki uniform.

By 1970 or 1971 VNMC units were using U.S. Army style body armor with the collar.

VNMC equipment in the early 1950s was still basically French but was replaced with older U.S. webbed gear, ammo pouches, etc. By the late 1960s modern U.S. M-56 gear was coming into general use.

VNMC rank insignia was the same as that used in the Vietnamese Navy except Army designations were used (i.e. though the rank insignia of an ensign was worn he would be designated as a second lieutenant). In the case of officers and higher ranking sergeants, rank was worn on a blue tag attached to one of the upper buttons on the utilities. On khaki uniforms rank was on shoulder boards. These tags or shoulder boards were blue with yellow markings. Ranks ran as follows: 2nd lieutenant – one narrow stripe with a curl, 1st lieutenant – two narrow stripes and a curl, captain – three narrow stripes and a curl, major – two wide stripes and a curl, lieutenant colonel – three wide stripes and a curl, and colonel – four wide stripes and a curl. NCOs rank was either designated by point up chevrons and a curl worn on tags for higher ranking sergeants or down slanting chevrons for lower ranking NCOs.

By about 1956 standard armament for the VNMC was the American M1 Carbine. Heavier weapons included the BAR, .30 Browning MG, and 81 mm. mortar. In 1959 marksmanship training was given more stress in the VNMC and to allow higher standards to be achieved the M1 Garand replaced the M1 Carbine. In 1967 the Vietnamese Marines were among the first Republic of Vietnam troops equipped with the M16 rifle which along with the M79 grenade launcher, M60 GPMG, and M72 LAW anti-tank weapon, they used for the rest of the war.

The Vietnamese Air Force

The VNAF was formed in 1951 as part of the French Air Force, but the first Vietnamese squadron was not really formed until 1954. In mid 1954 the VNAF had 58 aircraft and about 1350 personnel. By 1956 the VNAF had grown to a strength of 4140 men manning an F-8F fighter squadron, two C-47 transport squadrons, two L-19 squadrons, and some H-19 helicopters. Jet aircraft were prohibited by the Geneva Agreements.

During the remainder of the 1950s there was little change in the composition of the VNAF, but in an effort to improve South Vietnamese ability to combat the Communist insurgents, in 1960 25 U.S. Navy AD-6 fighters were shipped to Vietnam to replace the F-8Fs. The U.S.A. also furnished the VNAF with 11 H-34 helicopters. To help man these new aircraft VNAF strength rose to about 4600 in 1960. In 1961 President Kennedy approved additional U.S. aid to the VNAF. As a result plans were made for a second VNAF fighter squadron, a third L-19 squadron, and a photo recon unit. Arrangements were made to lend the VNAF 30 T-28 aircraft for the new fighter squadron, and by April, 1962, it was operational. Vietnamese ground crews were also trained to service T-28s. In September, 1962, the VNAF activated its first reconnaissance squadron, the 716th at Tan Son Nhut on two RC-45s.

By 1963 the VNAF was flying an average of 800–900 tactical sorties per month, but still they could not respond to all requests for air support. The next year Air Force strength grew to 11,000, and General Nguyen Cao Ky – a competent and dynamic leader who in 1965 was to become premier – had taken over the command of the VNAF. The year 1964 also saw the decision made to equip a new VNAF squadron with A-1Hs. Later, this single squadron was increased to four squadrons to be equipped with A-1Hs. During November–December, 1964, the USAF and VNAF inflicted an estimated 2500 enemy casualties.

Attacks were launched against installations in North Vietnam by the USAF and VNAF on 8 February 1965. General Ky himself led one of the VNAF raiding units. Later in 1965, however, the VNAF stopped flying missions against the North to concentrate on flying support missions within South Vietnam. During 1965 and 1966 the VNAF continued to grow gradually, and Vietnamese pilots flew support missions along with USAF and USMC pilots.

By 1967 VNAF strength was around 16,000, and in June of that year the VNAF 522nd Fighter Squadron became active flying F-5 Freedom

Fighters. In early 1968 at the start of the Tet Offensive, the VNAF boasted 362 aircraft and 16,277 personnel. Principal VNAF strike aircraft – despite the jet squadron – was still the A–1. Between 30 January and 25 February, at the height of the Tet Offensive, aircraft from the VNAF flew 4648 close air support sorties, 1535 interdiction sorties, 216 reconnaissance sorties, and 814 airlift sorties.

By May, 1969, three squadrons – the 524th, 520th, and 516th Fighter Squadrons – had each replaced their A-1s with 18 A-37Bs. As 1969 closed VNAF strength approached 36,000.

By 1970 as the USAF began its pullout, the VNAF had expanded even more to fill the void, 40,000 VNAF personnel staffing nine tactical wings. The VNAFs inventory of 700 planes. During 1970 the VNAF flew strike missions both within South Vietnam and in support of the move into Cambodia. Some 28,249 attack sorties were flown by the VNAF during the year.

VNAF responsibility grew even more in 1971 as Vietnamese pilots flew 70 per cent. of all combat missions during that year. By the end of 1971 VNAF strength was approaching 42,000 deployed into 44 squadrons.

When the North Vietnamese launched their invasion in March, 1972, the VNAF had over 1350 aircraft available. Between 31 March and 30 April, 1972, the VNAF flew 4651 close air support sorties, 340 interdiction sorties, 474 reconnaissance sorties, and 863 airlift sorties. Eventually, most of the ground lost to the North Vietnamese attackers was regained with the help of massive USAF and VNAF support. The VNAF flew 40,000 strike sorties during 1972.

In the years between 1972 and 1975 the Republic of Vietnam based a large part of its strategic and tactical planning on the strength of its air force. Though American cutbacks in aid affected the VNAF and caused the disbandment of 11 squadrons, the VNAF could still muster 1673 aircraft in 55 squadrons and was staffed by 63,000 personnel when the North Vietnamese offensive began in 1975. The VNAF found that the large numbers of SAMs and AA employed by the NVA caused heavy losses in aircraft. Still, the VNAF flew over 7500 sorties between 10 March and 10 April, 1975, and some Air Force units such as those at Phu Cat and Phan Rang fought heroically. Overall, though, as morale declined so did the effectiveness of the VNAF which ceased to exist as an effective force with the fall of Bien Hoa and Tan Son Nhut.

Uniforms and Equipment

Vietnamese Air Force personnel wore a wide variety of head gear, though not as wide as the ARVN. The standard service hat was blue and resembled the one in use with USAF personnel. VNAF cap insignia was worn on the front. VNAF pilots, who normally were trained by USAF pilots, wore headgear similar to their American mentors. These included Air Commando style hats, baseball type hats, and white flying helmets. A beret which the author has only seen in black and white photos was also sometimes worn early in the war. It appears to resemble the Army khaki or tan beret. VNAF ground crewmen sometimes wore the same baseball type utility hats used by USAF personnel but with different colors indicating assignment to different ground crew functions.

The dress uniform for officers consisted of a blue tunic or jacket worn out over blue trousers. This four button tunic had two breast pockets and two side pockets. A black tie and white shirt were normally worn with this coat. Pilots wore their wings, which were silver and consisted of a winged star, on the left breast. Rank insignia was worn on shoulder boards. The enlisted dress uniform consisted of an 'Ike' jacket and trousers of the same style as those worn by officers. Both were blue in color. The jacket had two breast pockets and three buttons down the front. Senior NCOs wore their rank insignia on shoulder boards and junior NCOs wore theirs on the sleeves.

Other uniforms worn by the VNAF included a tan light weight uniform consisting of shirt and trousers, green utilities similar to those worn by the USAF, and flying suits of NOMEX or other material. These suits were often duplicates of USAF flight suits, having pockets for pens, etc. on the upper sleeves and zipped pockets on the legs. VNAF pilots often wore colorful scarves with their flying suits. High ranking pilots such as General Ky would frequently wear custom-tailored flight suits.

Low quarter black dress shoes were usually worn with the blue dress uniform or the khakis, while black high top combat or flying boots were standard with the flight suit or with utilities.

Much as did USAF pilots, VNAF pilots often wore three or four insignia on their flight suits. In addition to one or two squadron and/or wing patches on the breast, VNAF pilots often wore a shoulder patch on the left arm showing what type of airplane they were 'driving'. These were patterned after the same types of patches worn by USAF personnel. VNAF ground crews usually wore squadron or unit insignia on the breast of their utilities and sometimes wore some type of patch indicating whether they were an engine mechanic, radar technician, armament technician, etc. The VNAF pocket insignia consisting of a winged dragon on a shield was normally worn with most uniforms.

VNAF officers rank was indicated by the following insignia: lieutenant general – four stars; major general – three stars; brigadier general – two stars; and sub-brigadier general – one star. It should be noted that the arrangement of the stars was different from that for U.S. generals. A colonel wore three silver plum blossoms; a lieutenant colonel two silver plum blossoms; a major one silver plum blossom; a captain three gold plum blossoms; a first lieutenant two gold plum blossoms, and a second lieutenant one gold plum blossom. A student officer wore a single gold button or disk and an air cadet wore a gold button and a chevron with a curl. On shoulder boards a master sergeant wore a single silver button with a horizontal stripe; a sergeant first class wore three silver chevrons; and a sergeant wore one silver chevron. On the neck side of both officers and sergeants shoulder boards was a gold winged star. On the sleeve a corporal first class wore two gold and one silver chevrons over a winged gold star; a corporal two gold chevrons over the winged star; and an airman first class one gold chevron over the winged star. An airman second class wore just the gold winged star without chevrons.

Standard weapon among VNAF pilots was normally a S & W .38 Special revolver. Many Vietnamese pilots tried to obtain 2 inch barreled revolvers which were easier to carry on their smaller frames and which also carried more status. Survival knives and other survival equipment similar to that used by USAF pilots were also normally carried.

The Vietnamese Navy

Although the Vietnamese Navy was officially established in March, 1952, it took until well into 1953 before officers and crews could be trained

and ships acquired for them to man. The first unit of the VNN was activated in April, 1953. This unit was a 'dinassaut' consisting of five landing craft armed with .50 MGs and 20 mm. automatic guns. Another VNN 'dinassaut' was formed later in the year. Both, however, were still partially manned by French cadres and were commanded by French officers.

In February, 1954, the VNN received three minesweepers from the French, and in March and August two more 'dinassauts' were formed. In 1955 complete control of these units was turned over to the South Vietnamese.

By early 1956 the Vietnamese Navy had grown to a strength of 2160 men. Despite the establishment of a 'deep water' force, though, the VNN remained basically a riverine and coastal navy. By the end of 1956 VNN strength had reached 3371. The River Force was divided into six 'dinassauts' based at My Tho, Cat Lo, Vinh Long, Cat Lai, Can Tho, and Lang Xuyen. The greatest deficiency of the Vietnamese Navy remained its lack of qualified technical and repair personnel, a lack that was being remedied by sending officers and NCOs to foreign technical courses.

By early 1957 the first Vietnamese naval personnel trained in the U.S.A. had returned to act as instructors in Vietnamese naval schools. During 1958 and 1959 the VNN grew slowly, reaching a strength of 3600 men by 1959.

As of 1960 the Vietnamese fleet consisted of the following craft: 5 submarine chasers, 3 coastal minesweepers, 2 auxiliary motor minesweepers, 4 LSMs, 2 LSSLs (Support Landing Ship, Large), 5 LSILs (Landing Ship, Infantry Large), 7 LCUs (Landing Craft, Utility), 67 LCMs (Landing Craft, Mechanized, used as light mortar or gunboats on riverine operations), 111 LCVPs (Landing Craft, Vehicle, Personnel), and 1 fleet oiler. In addition there were various other small craft. To man this growing fleet, the VNN had about 4300 personnel by late 1960.

Between 1960 and 1964 VNN strength almost tripled, nearing the 12,000 mark. Much of this additional strength was needed to man the small patrol boats required to cover the VC infested Mekong Delta region. The increased number of American ships patrolling off of the coast of South Vietnam by 1964 limited the need for development of the South Vietnamese Navy's deep water capability.

By 1966 when U.S. Navy riverine forces were committed to the Delta the VNN numbered over 15,800 men. In the Mekong Delta – the 4th Naval

Vietnamese members of a dinassaut parade in front of their vessel. The jumper, canvas leggings, etc. are very similar to those worn by French Marine Fusiliers.

Zone – were six river assault groups and eleven coastal groups. These coastal groups were usually known as the 'Junk Force' or 'Junk Fleet' because of the number of motorized junks they employed. VNN riverine forces were used to patrol and to transport ARVN and Ruff Puff units in the Delta area.

In the years 1966–69 U.S. riverine operations assumed prime importance in the Mekong Delta, though VNN personnel worked closely with the USN in patrolling and attacking enemy positions. In 1967 strength was just over 16,000, up barely 200 from 1966. By the end of 1968, though, it was approaching 19,000. In 1969 training facilities were strained as the VNN was rapidly increased to the 30,000 level, a result at

least in part from the U.S. Navy turning over a large number of river craft to the VNN during the first half of 1969, used in support of the VNMC and ARVN and also as part of the U.S./Vietnamese 'Sea Lords' program of interdiction of enemy water supply routes.

As U.S. forces began pulling out, the VNN continued to expand rapidly in both ships and men to enable the Vietnamese to take over patrol responsibility from the USN. By the 1972 Communist invasion there were over 42,000 men in the VNN providing crews for over 1500 craft of all sizes.

In 1973 major craft of the South Vietnamese fleet included: 7 frigates; 2 destroyer escorts; 3 PCEs (patrol craft, 2 of which were used as rescue ships); 5 MSFs (minesweepers); 20 patrol gunboats; 26 coast guard cutters; 2 coastal minesweepers; 6 LSTs, 6 LSMs, 4 LSSLs, 5 LSILs, and more than a thousand smaller craft including 107 swiftboats, 293 PBRs, 42 river monitors, 22 LCM monitors, 100 ATCs, and 250 motor junks. The VNN was still primarily a coastal and river force, but it ranked as one of the most powerful navies in the third world.

As it turned out, the South Vietnamese Navy did not get a chance to play much of a part in the defense of South Vietnam during April, 1975. In some cases VNN craft provided fire support, but the primary contribution made by the VNN was in evacuating troops and their dependants from the northern provinces and later from the Republic of Vietnam itself.

Uniforms and Equipment

Standard dress headgear for VNN officers and petty officers was a white service hat with a black bill. Officers wore a silver band and petty officers a gold band just above the bill. Both wore a cap badge bearing crossed anchors (a later badge bore only a single anchor). These same ranks also wore a khaki service hat similar to that worn by U.S. Navy officers and petty officers. The khaki hat was used for everyday service wear. VNN seamen wore a white 'Dixie Cup' sailors hat similar to that worn in the U.S. Navy. Members of the riverine and junk forces frequently wore a black beret bearing a circular badge with a stylized junk in the middle. At least a few junk force crewmen also wore green berets bearing this badge, but they may have served on craft forming part of the U.S. Special Forces' own junk force. Vietnamese SEALs wore a beret badge bearing bullion wings, wreath, shield, and anchor.

Standard dress uniform for officers and petty officers in the VNN was a blue double-breasted coat, having two rows of three gold buttons worn over a white shirt and black tie with blue trousers. For everyday wear a khaki uniform consisting of shirt and trousers was worn. Seamen normally wore a white 'middy' blouse with white sailors collar edged with triple blue stripes. A black sailors-knot tie was worn with this blouse. Green utilities were sometimes worn for everyday shipboard duties, though at least a few Vietnamese

sailors were also issued American style dungarees. Junk force crewmen often wore just a pair of black 'pajama' bottoms. VNN SEALs – the LDNN (Lin Dei Nugel Nghai) wore American scuba equipment, etc.

Dress shoes were black low quarters, but seamen and many petty officers wore sandals or sneakers or even went barefoot aboard junks and riverine craft.

VNN flag ranks were designated by the following insignia: Admiral of the Fleet – five stars on black shoulder boards. Admiral – four stars on black shoulder boards; Vice Admiral – three stars on black shoulder boards; Rear Admiral – two stars on black shoulder boards; Commodore – one star on black shoulder boards.

Other officers ranks were indicated by gold stripes on the lower sleeve as follows: Captain – four wide stripes, the top one with a curl; Commander – three wide stripes with a curl; Lieutenant Commander – two wide stripes with a curl; Lieutenant – three narrow stripes with a curl; Lieutenant (JG) – two narrow stripes with a curl; Ensign – one narrow stripe with a curl; Aspirant – one narrow stripe with a curl and a red bar at each side.

Petty Officers wore black shoulder boards bearing gold stripes or chevrons as follows: Chief Warrant Officer – one wide gold stripe with a curl and two narrow stripes; Warrant Officer – one wide stripe with a curl and two narrow stripes; Petty Officer First Class – three narrow chevrons, the top one with a curl; Petty Officer Second Class – two narrow chevrons with a curl. Seamens ranks were designated with chevrons worn on the sleeve: Specialist – three chevrons (navy blue, sky blue, navy blue); Leading Seaman – three navy blue chevrons; Able Seaman – two navy blue chevrons; Seaman – one navy blue chevron. Later in the war these insignia were changed to more closely resemble those worn by U.S. Navy personnel. Other insignia worn by the VNN included specialists badges. The Navy ordnance badge, for example, was a small nickeled badge just under 2 inches in diameter depicting a bomb, anchor, and lightning bolts.

Junk Force and riverine force troops from the VNN were usually equipped with the same small arms as the other Vietnamese services. M1 and M2 Carbines predominated until 1968 or 1969 when they were replaced by M16s. M60 GPMGs and M79 grenade launchers also saw some use with the VNN.

8 Allied Forces in Vietnam

The Republic of Korea

By 1968, the Republic of Korea was supplying 75 per cent. of Free World Military Assistance Forces in Vietnam. Anyone who served with a ROK unit soon learned, too, that the Korean troops were tough with a capital 'T'. Just moving a ROK battalion into an area was normally enough to secure it.

The first group of 128 Koreans, comprising a MASH and a group of Taekwando instructors, arrived in Vietnam in September, 1964. Between February and June, 1965, 2416 additional Korean troops designated the Korean Military Assistance Group, Vietnam, were deployed. Nicknamed the 'Dove Unit', this group consisted of engineering troops from the Army and Marines, naval support craft and crews, and an Army security company. Later in 1965 an Army transport company, more engineers, a service unit, and a liaison group were added to the Korean forces, and the security unit was increased to battalion strength.

The really major Korean commitment began in September, 1965, when the HQ of the ROK Capital Division (also known as the 'Tiger Division') arrived at Qui Nhon. By the end of the year two of the division's regiments – the 1st Infantry Regiment and the Cavalry Regiment – had taken up positions near Qui Nhon where they could patrol along Highway 19 and defend the key logistical area around Qui Nhon. Although the Capital Division was short one regiment, this lack was more than compensated for by the deployment of the ROK 2nd Marine Brigade (the 'Blue Dragons') in October, 1965. The 'Blue Dragons' were originally assigned to security duty at Cam Ranh Bay. By the end of 1965, more than 20,000 ROK troops were in Vietnam.

During 1966, the Capital Division began to expand its control north from Qui Nhon to Phu Cat mountain and west along Highway 19. In January, 1966, the ROKs had already shown how well they could fight, too, having killed 192 VC while losing only 11 ROKs during Operation 'Flying Tiger'. Reinforcements in the form of the 26th Infantry Regiment arrived in April. By September, a second ROK Division – the 9th 'White Horse' Division – had been deployed into the area near Ninh Hoa, where they could control Highway 1. The 'White Horse' HQ was in Ninh Hoa while the 28th Regiment was around Tuy Hoa, the 29th Regiment around Ninh Hoa, and the 30th Regiment west of Cam Ranh Bay.

With two Army divisions and a Marine brigade in Vietnam, the ROKs had established a corps level HQ in Nha Trang under the command of Major General Chae Myung Shin. In addition to the five infantry regiments, cavalry regiment, and

Member of the ROK Special Forces teaches Rappelling techniques to Recondo students. He wears a tiger patch (for which reason the ROK Special Forces troops were sometimes called 'Tigers') and his jump wings on his black beret.

Marine brigade, there were ROK artillery, engineer, transportation, signal, and service battalions as well as armor, recon, MP, medical, ordnance, quartermaster, and aviation companies assigned to the ROK divisions or corps. Special units included Special Forces, intelligence, and 'psy ops'.

Later in 1966, the ROKs were involved in two major operations in the II Corps area. The Capital Division under the command of General Lew Byong Hion was involved in 'Haeng Ho 6' in Binh Dinh Province. Elements of the Capital Division were also assisting the 1st Air Cavalry Division in Operation 'Irving' in Binh Dinh Province. In August, the ROK 2nd Marine Brigade had moved to I Corps. By the end of 1966, 45,566 ROK troops were serving in Vietnam.

In 1967, one additional ROK Marine battalion and additional support troops were despatched to Vietnam. On 7 March, the ROKs began their largest operation to date with 'Oh Jac Kyo I.'

During this year, as they would throughout the war, the ROKs inflicted enormous casualties on the enemy by comparison with those they suffered. Kill ratios of 20 to 1 or higher were the norm with the ROKs. They also tended to

Members of the ROK 9th Division arrive at Nha Trang in September, 1966. Rank insignia is worn on the helmets, which do not have camo covers.

ANZAC FORCES

Royal Australian Regiment Trooper This trooper wears Australian issue utilities, boonie hat, boots, and webbed gear, the magazine pouches being designed to accommodate magazines for the L1A1 self-loading rifle with which he is equipped. **Australian Special Air Service Warrant Officer** This member of the SAS wears U.S. leaf pattern camo and U.S. jungle boots. His crown (Class II) is worn on the left sleeve. The black beret indicates he is one of the SAS advisors to the ARVN Hac Baos (Black Panthers). The weapon is a captured AK47. **New Zealand Special Air Service Trooper** This Maori of the NZSAS wears leaf pattern utilities with an OD towel around his neck. His headgear is one of the varied types of boonie hat ubiquitous in Vietnam. Much of his gear is U.S. issue – including the M203 version of the M16 rifle with 40 mm grenade launcher below the barrel – but he retains the SAS issue Bergen rucksack.

ANZAC FORCES

Royal Australian Regiment Trooper

New Zealand Special Air Service Trooper

Australian Special Air Service Warrant
Officer, Advisor to ARVN Hac Baos

capture a very large number of enemy weapons, usually an even truer test of efficiency in Vietnam than body count.

The last part of 1967 the ROKs devoted to aggressive patrolling along Highways 1 and 19 and to providing security for elections which took place in September. Late in the year, however, the Capital Division did commence Operation 'Maeng Ho 9' in Binh Dinh Province.

In 1968, the ROKs continued to concentrate mostly on patrolling and search and destroy

Men of the Tiger Division check their position during August, 1969. Note the Tiger Division shoulder patch and what appears to be branch insignia on the collar of the man at the right.

Men of the ROK Tiger Division arrive in Vietnam in May, 1966. Note the brightly patterned camo cover worn on the helmet, the shoulder patch, and the M1/M2 carbines carried.

operations in their area of responsibility. The Koreans were especially adept at surrounding and eliminating enemy units following contacts.

Some idea of the intensive patrolling by the ROKs can be gained from the fact that as 1968 ended, ROK troops were involved in 195 small unit operations. 1968 also marked the peak of ROK strength with just over 50,000 troops in Vietnam.

In 1969, the ROKs continued to put their greatest stress on small unit patrols and search and destroy operations. So effective were their cordon and search operations that the enemy rarely escaped from them and kill ratios ran as high as 100 to 1. Most ROK operations were of regimental size or less in 1969.

During 1970, the ROKs continued to conduct an average of 150 small unit operations per day. During 1971 and 1972, the ROKs were involved in less actions, though they continued to patrol

while turning responsibility for the defense of their area over to ARVN units. The 1st and 2nd Battalions of the Marine brigade left in December, 1971, and the remaining two Marine battalions left in January and February, 1972. Both the Capital and 9th Divisions remained 'in country' until March, 1973.

The general consensus among any U.S. troops who saw the ROKs in action was that they were tough and well-disciplined. At times their careful and methodical planning of operations frustrated MACV planners who felt the Koreans stood down for too long between major operations. However, on the positive side the ROKs were outstanding at company sized search and destroy, search and clear, or ambush operations.

Troops from the ROK 26th Regiment assigned to the Tiger Division are instructed about booby traps. Note the jungle boots, multiple canteens, and M16 rifles.

The Korean government had made it a point to send crack units to Vietnam, and every ROK soldier or Marine was a volunteer. Other units had been combed for top officers and NCOs to serve with the Tigers and White Horses. As a result of these high selection standards the average ROK trooper was very physically fit and highly motivated. Probably the most commonly uttered evaluation of the ROKs by the average grunt was, 'God, I'm glad they're on our side!' And, that is a pretty fair comment on the fighting reputation of the Koreans in Vietnam.

Uniforms and Equipment

As did most allied units in Vietnam, the ROKs wore primarily U.S. style uniforms and equipment. The basic headgear was an olive drab utility hat or an M-1 style steel helmet with camouflage cover and often – as with U.S. troops – a rubber band around it. The ROKs, however, were too 'squared away' to tuck things into their helmet bands. Officers wore rank insignia on the front of their utility caps. The ROKs mounted very sharp honor guards which normally wore a nickeled or chromed helmet liner. Members of the ROK Special Forces wore a black beret, often with airborne wings affixed as a beret badge. ROK Marines wore the same OD utility cap or combat helmet as the Army.

The basic ROK uniform was green utilities, though the ROK Special Forces wore a distinctive type of spotted camouflage utilities. Normally, the ROKs did not wear flak jackets, though there may, of course, have been some exceptions. One other uniform seen in wear relatively often with the ROKs was the judo or karate gi consisting of a heavily woven jacket and light cotton pants. A good percentage of the ROKs wore the black belt with their gis.

Standard boots were black combat boots of U.S. style. For ceremonial occasions these might be worn with white shoe laces. Some Koreans were issued the U.S. pattern jungle boot.

ROK webbed gear was of U.S. pattern, but in the earlier part of the war tended to be of the older style since the ROKs were still armed with M1 or M2 carbines or M1 Garands and were using the bandoliers or pouches designed for use with the magazines for these weapons. The ROKs usually traveled fairly light in the field, but they did carry as many as three canteens on their pistol belts. Since the magazine pouches normally worn on the M-56 gear could also be used for M1 or M2 carbine magazines the date at which M-56 gear became widely distributed is not certain, but by the late 1960s most ROK units were equipped with M-56 harness.

Normally, rank insignia was worn on the collars for officers and on the arm for NCOs. Although ROK generals used the same system of stars as U.S. generals, other officers were designated by either diamonds or eight-pointed stars. Warrant officers wore a single gold diamond; a 2nd lieutenant a single silver diamond; a 1st lieutenant two silver diamonds; and a captain three silver diamonds. A major wore one eight-pointed star; a lt col. two eight-pointed stars; and a colonel three eight-pointed stars. NCOs chevrons were red; corporals, privates first class and privates wearing half chevrons. Divisional insignia was worn on the left sleeve. The Capital Division wore a patch bearing a brightly colored tiger, while the 9th Division wore a circular patch bearing a rampant white horse on a black background. Rating badges, parachutists wings, etc, were sometimes worn on the left breast. What appears to be branch insignia seems to be worn on the left collar in some photographs as well.

In the early war years, the basic ROK individual weapon was the M1 or M2 carbine, but was later replaced by the M16. The Colt 1911A1 .45 pistol was the basic sidearm, but Korean generals often preferred Smith & Wesson .38 special revolvers. Heavier weapons such as the .50 caliber MG, M-60 GPMG, etc. were also the same as those used by the U.S. Army.

Thailand

The earliest Thai contribution to the defense of South Vietnam was 16 members of the Royal Thai Air Force who arrived in September, 1964, for the purpose of flying and maintaining transport aircraft. The first increase in Thai personnel assigned to Vietnam came in 1966 when some additional airmen arrived to fly and maintain C-47s and C-123s, but the real Thai contribution began in 1967.

During the early months of 1967 there were discussions about the size of the unit to be sent, and it was finally decided to send a regimental combat team of about 3300 troops. The unit chosen was the 'Queen's Cobras', a crack infantry formation. The unit was organized into an HQ company with a communications platoon, an

Above:
The Koreans were well-known for turning out smart color guards such as this one from the White Horse Div. The unit shoulder patch bears a rampant white horse.

Above left:
ROK Marine LTC (right) inspects the weapon of a member of the ROK 2nd Marine Bn. USMC style fatigue hat is worn by the officer. As with U.S. Marines, the ROK Marines also wore green fatigues with camo helmet cover.

Two ROK generals watch a Taekwondo demonstration. The general on the left wears U.S. parachutist's wings. Note also the Tiger Division insignia and the short barreled S & W revolver worn by the general on the right.

Members of the Thai 'Black Panther' Division arrive in Saigon in July, 1968. Equipment is similar to that in use with U.S. troops. The U.S. Naval uniforms are worn by the crewmen of the transport ship.

U.S. major general presenting awards to members of Thai armed forces serving in Vietnam. Note subdued 'Thailand' and 'Royal Thai Army' tabs, and U.S. style helmets and covers.

aviation platoon, an M-113 platoon, a 'psy ops' platoon, a heavy weapons platoon (MG section and 81 mm. mortar section), a service company (personnel, special service, supply and transport, maintenance, and military police platoons), four rifle companies, a reinforced combat engineer company, a medical company, a cavalry recon troop (two recon platoons and an M-113 platoon), and a 105 mm. howitzer battery.

The 'Cobras' were fully deployed by September, serving with the U.S. 9th Infantry Division at Bear Cat. By October, the 'Cobras' were already in action participating in Operation 'Narasuan' in Bien Hoa province where they killed 145 of the enemy. The Thais, being fellow Southeast Asians, proved very effective in civic action projects such as medical aid to local populations. Thai naval personnel also served during 1967 manning coastal patrol craft.

Member of the Queen's Cobras with an M2 guards equipment in the Republic of Vietnam during July, 1967.

It had been decided in 1967 to increase the Thai forces in Vietnam to divisional strength. Deployment of this unit began in July, 1968, when the Thai HQ, Vietnam, was increased from 35 to 228 men. Approximately one-half of the Thai Division (5700 men) arrived in July, 1968. As this initial increment of the 'Black Panthers' arrived, the 'Queen's Cobras' rotated back to Thailand in August, 1968.

By late February, 1969, the second increment of the Thai division – 5704 men – had arrived in South Vietnam, to be followed in August by the final increment. This final group of troops actually consisted of a replacement brigade for the first contingent of 'Black Panthers' which had arrived in July, 1968, and which was rotated back to Thailand.

At full strength, the 'Black Panther' Division was made up of 11,266 troops which included an overstrength of 5 per cent. Divisional strength was broken down as follows: a divisional HQ and HQ company, two infantry brigades each of 2867 troops (a brigade HQ and HQ company and three infantry battalions), a reconnaissance battalion with a strength of 660 men (HQ and HQ troop, LRRP company, and three mechanized infantry troops), divisional artillery (artillery HQ and HQ battery, two 105 mm. howitzer batteries, and one 155 mm. howitzer battery), a signals battalion, an aviation company, an engineer battalion (engineer HQ and HQ company and two engineer companies), and an MP company. These units were backed up by a 1246 man support group.

The Thai area of responsibility was an agricultural province, hence security for the harvests and search and clear operations were their primary missions.

During 1970, Thai troop strength increased slightly to a high of 11,586, at least partially due to additional Thai airmen added to the 'Victory Flight'. Plans were, however, made in 1970 to withdraw most Thai combat units during the following year. In the summer of 1970 the 'Black Panther' Division was redesignated the Royal Thai Army Volunteer Force.

During August, 1971, one brigade of the RTAVF was returned to Thailand and was not replaced. By December, 1972, Thai Air Force and Naval personnel had left Vietnam as well. In January and February, 1972, most remaining combat troops of the RTAVF left Vietnam, all elements being gone by March.

The Thais sent the second largest force of any allied nation, and these were elite troops at that. Less obvious, but just as important, is the fact that Thailand was another Southeast Asian nation sending aid.

Uniforms and Equipment

As with many other allies in Vietnam, the Thais were basically equipped with U.S. equipment.

The two most commonly worn pieces of Thai headgear in Vietnam were an OD utility cap similar to the U.S. 'baseball' style utility hat and the M-1 steel helmet with camouflage cover. For dress wear, a service hat similar to that of the American or other Western nations was worn, for officers bearing a cap badge consisting of gold and red sun with a gold Thai crown on a red disk. The enlisted cap badge lacked the sun's rays.

For field use, OD utilities similar to those worn by U.S. troops were normally issued. Tiger striped camouflage utilities were sometimes used

LTG Do Cau Tri affixes a Vietnamese unit citation streamer to the colors of the Thai Black Panther Division in July, 1969.

by LRRPs or other special troops. Reportedly some Thai LRRPs also favored utilities which had been dyed black or of indigenous camouflage patterns made in Thailand. The dress uniform was somewhat British in appearance consisting of an OD coat or tunic and trousers. The tunic was belted and was worn over a light olive shirt with an OD tie.

Black American style combat boots were standard with the Thais, though jungle boots were later issued to Thai personnel. Black dress shoes were worn with the dress uniform.

Equipment once again tended to be of U.S. pattern. In the early days of Thai participation in Vietnam older style U.S. webbed gear, combat suspenders, pouches, etc. were used along with the older metal canteens. Later, more modern M-56 harness and the accompanying canteens, first aid pouches, magazine pouches, entrenching tool, rucksack, etc. came into use.

On their combat uniforms the Thais wore two or three distinguishing insignia. On the left shirt pocket was worn a tape bearing 'Royal Thai Army' and on the left shoulder was worn either a tab bearing 'THAILAND' or a shield shaped patch bearing red, white, and blue stripes and a 'THAILAND' tab. Airborne qualified personnel (many of whom fought in Laos on clandestine operations), pilots, etc. sometimes wore a cloth version of their qualification badges on their breast. With the dress uniform, branch of service badges were worn on the lapels of the tunic.

Officers rank was indicated as follows: 2nd lieutenant – one star; 1st lieutenant – two stars ; captain – three stars; major – a Thai crown; lieutenant colonel – a Thai crown and one star; colonel – a Thai crown and two stars; brigadier general – a crown and a wreath; major general – a crown, a wreath, and a star; lieutenant general – a crown, a wreath, and two stars. Warrant officers wore an insignia bearing crossed swords. NCOs were designated as follows: master sergeant – three chevrons and a bar; sergeant 1st class – two chevrons and a bar; staff sergeant – one chevron

Member of the 'Queen's Cobra' Regiment of the Royal Thai Army takes cover during a mission near the village of Phocu Tho. Utilities, helmet cover and boots are typical of members of the 'Cobras' c. 1967. Weapon is the M79 grenade launcher and flak jacket is U.S. Army issue.

In 1965 Australian ground combat troops were deployed to Vietnam. The first to arrive were the 1st Battalion, Royal Australian Regiment (RAR) who were 'in country' by the end of May. This battalion was attached to the U.S. 173rd Airborne Brigade at Bien Hoa. Also arriving with the 1st Battalion, RAR were about 100 more 'jungle warfare specialists'.

Among other Australian units arriving during 1965 were the 1st Armored Personnel Carrier (APC) Troop; 527th Signal Troop; 105th Field Artillery Battery; 709th Signal Troop; a logistics support company; and 3rd Field Troop; 1st Field Squadron. By the end of 1965, over 1500 Australians were serving in Vietnam. HQ, Australian Army Force, Vietnam had been established in Saigon during May.

In 1966, Australian strength tripled, topping 4500 by the end of the year. The 5th and 6th Battalions, RAR, arrived 'in country' in April, and the 1st Battalion left in June. Also arriving in April were the 1st APC Squadron (which incorporated the 1st APC Troop); the 1st Field Artillery Regiment (minus one battery); the 1st Field Squadron (which incorporated the 3rd Field Troop); the 3rd SAS Squadron (minus one troop); the 21st Engineer Support Troop; the 103rd Signal Squadron; the 506th, 520th, 552nd, and 581st Signal Troops; the HQ, 145th Signal Squadron; the 1st Australian Logistics Support Group; the 55th Engineer Workshop and Park Squadron (minus some elements); the 17th Construction Squadron (minus one troop); and the 1st Royal Australian Army Service Company. With the arrival of these additional units and some additional RAAF and RAN personnel, the HQ at Saigon was upgraded to HQ, Australian Forces, Vietnam. The 1st Australian Task Force was also established in April with HQ at Nui Dat about 35 miles southeast of Saigon. The ATF was given Phuoc Tuy Province as its area of responsibility.

During 1967, the 2nd and 7th Battalions, RAR, arrived to replace the 5th and 6th Battalions which left in July. In January, the 1st APC Squadron was redesignated A Squadron, 3rd Cavalry Regiment. Later, in March, the 1st SAS Squadron (less one troop) arrived to replace the 3rd SAS Squadron which departed in July.

and a bar; sergeant – three chevrons with a Thai crown; corporal – two chevrons with Thai crown; lance corporal – one chevron with Thai crown.

The Thais were armed with U.S. weapons. Originally, there were not enough M16s available so the 'Queen's Cobras' were issued M2 carbines. As the M16 became available in quantity, though, the Thais were re-armed with M16s. Higher ranking Thai officers often affected 2 inch barreled Smith & Wesson revolvers as did many Asian generals or colonels. The M79 grenade launcher and M60 GPMG were among the other widely used light infantry weapons.

Australia

The first Australian troops arrived in Vietnam during July, 1962, when 30 advisors from the Australian Army Training Team, Vietnam (AATTV), many of whom were jungle warfare specialists from the Australian Special Air Service, began training Vietnamese troops.

Also in March, the 4th Field Artillery Regiment (minus one battalion) arrived to replace the 1st Field Artillery Regiment which departed in July. Other units arriving in March included 1st Civil Affairs Unit; 104th Signal Squadron; HQ, 110th Signal Squadron; 532nd, 547th, 557th, 561st, and 704th Signal Troops; and 5th Royal Australian Army Service Company.

Additional units leaving in July included the 506th, 520th, 527th, and 581st Signal Troops; the HQ of the 145th Signal Squadron; and the 1st

Australian SAS officer serving with a MIKE Force company makes radio contact. Note the tiger striped camouflage uniforms and the much worn and assorted types of boonie hats. A MIKE Force member on the right wears a U.S. 101st Airborne patch on his pocket.

Royal Australian Army Service Company. In November, the 503rd, 532nd, 557th, 561st, 704th, and 709th Signal Troops were absorbed into the 110th Signal Squadron, and in December, the missing troop of the 1st Field Squadron arrived.

In the spring of 1967, the RAAF sent B-57 Canberra bombers to Phan Rang, and the RAN sent a destroyer – HMS *Hobart* – to Vietnamese waters. By the end of 1967, over 6800 Australian servicemen were in Vietnam.

During 1968, the number of RAR battalions 'in country' was increased to three, though at one point there were actually five battalions in Vietnam. The 1st Battalion returned to Vietnam in January, and the 4th Battalion arrived for its first tour in the same month. The 9th Battalion arrived in November. RAR battalions being redeployed during the year from Vietnam were the 2nd in June and the 3rd in December. Other units deployed to Vietnam during 1968 included: C Squadron, 1st Armored Regiment; 12th Field Artillery Regiment (less one battery); 2nd SAS Squadron (less one troop); and 26th Royal Australian Army Service Company. Additional units returning to Australia or being redeployed elsewhere during 1968 included: 4th Field Artillery Regiment in May and 1st SAS Squadron in February.

During 1969, Australian strength in Vietnam peaked at 7672. Among units arriving in Vietnam during 1969 were: 5th Battalion, RAR, in January; 8th Battalion, RAR, in November; B Squadron, 1st Armored Regiment, in February; B Squadron, 3rd Cavalry Regiment, in May; A Squadron, 1st Armored Regiment, in December; 1st Field Artillery Regiment in February; and 3rd SAS Squadron (less one troop) in February. Units leaving Vietnam during the year included: 1st Battalion, RAR, in February; 9th Battalion, RAR, in December; A Squadron, 3rd Cavalry Regiment, in May; C Squadron, 1st Armored Regiment, in February; B Squadron, 1st Armored Regiment, in December; 12th Field

Australian Warrant Officer attached to an ARVN Ranger unit (note maroon beret and Ranger beret badge) instructs in the use of the M79 grenade launcher. Note the WO's crown of the Australian Army Training Team Vietnam worn on the right sleeve and the 'Australia' tab on the shoulder loop. Although not always the case, most Australian WOs assigned to the ARVN Rangers were members of one of the Australian SAS Squadrons. Note the winged arrow on wreath beret badge of the ARVN Rangers.

Advisors from the Australian SAS (center) and U.S. Army Ranger (right) examine enemy weapons captured by Hac Bao (Black Panthers). Both men as well as the Vietnamese Ranger at the left wear black berets. The SAS man wears camouflage of U.S. pattern. Note the MACV patch on the left shoulder of the U.S. advisor, and the Black Panther beret badge worn on the berets. Though usually referred to as the strike company of the 1st ARVN Division, the Hac Bao advised by the two men illustrated was in reality a Ranger unit.

Artillery Regiment in March; and 2nd SAS Squadron in March. In early 1970, the 8th Battalion, RAR, saw quite a bit of action, winning a Vietnamese Cross of Gallantry for operations in the Long Hai Hills. Also in December men from the 3rd SAS Squadron made an operational parachute descent in eastern Phuoc Tuy Province, the first Australian combat jump in over 25 years.

In 1970 as the Australians began pulling troops out, special emphasis was given to training the 'Ruff Puffs' in Phuoc Tuy Province as part of Vietnamization. Although the aim was to lower the total number of Australian troops in Vietnam by the end of the year, new units continued to arrive in Vietnam during 1970. Less arrived, however, than departed. Units on strength in Vietnam in 1970 included: 7th Battalion, RAR, in February; 2nd Battalion, RAR, in April; C Squadron, 1st Armored Regiment, in December; 4th Field Artillery Regiment in February; and 1st SAS Squadron (less one troop) in February. All of these units were on their second tour in Vietnam. Those units being redeployed to Australia or elsewhere in 1970 included: 5th Battalion, RAR, in March; 6th Battalion, RAR, in May; 8th Battalion, RAR, in November; A Squadron, 1st Armored Regiment, in December; 1st Field Artillery Regiment in May; and 3rd SAS Squadron in February. Total Australian troop strength in Vietnam dropped to 6763 during 1970.

Men of the Thai Queen's Cobras on parade.

Member of the 6th Bn, Royal Australian Regiment on patrol in Phoc Tay Province. Uniform is typical of the RAR and rifle is the Australian version of the L1A1.

During 1971, the process of sending some new units to Vietnam while rotating home a larger number continued. Arriving in 1971 were: 3rd Battalion, RAR, in February; 4th Battalion, RAR, in May; A squadron, 3rd Cavalry Regiment, in January; 104th Field Artillery Battery in May; 12th Field Artillery Regiment in January; 2nd SAS Squadron (less one troop) in February; and the remainder of the 55th Engineer Workshop and Park Squadron in June. Most of these units had seen previous service in Vietnam, and most were to leave before 1971 ended. Units being redeployed from Vietnam in 1971 included: 7th Battalion, RAR, in March; 2nd Battalion, RAR, in June; 3rd Battalion, RAR, in October; B Squadron, 3rd Cavalry Regiment, in January; C Squadron, 1st Armored Regiment, in September; 104th Field Artillery Battery in December; 4th Field Artillery Regiment

in March; 12th Field Artillery Regiment in December; 1st Field Squadron in November; 1st SAS Squadron in February; 2nd SAS Squadron in October; 21st Engineer Support Troop in December; 1st Civil Affairs Unit in November; 104th Signal Squadron in December; 547th Signal Troop in December; 1st Australian Logistics Support Group in October; 26th Royal Australian Army Service Company in June; 176th AD Company in November; and 1st Australian Field Hospital in December. Many of the support units leaving in November and December had been assigned to the HQ, Australian Forces, Vietnam, or the HQ, 1st Australian Task Force. Actual combat units remaining as of the end of 1971 were one battalion of the Royal Australian Regiment and a cavalry squadron.

Most remaining Australians left Vietnam early

Men from the RAR firing an M60. Rounds for the GPMG are worn on belts around the torso in fashion which was typical in Vietnam.

in 1972. The 4th Battalion, RAR, pulled out in March as did A Squadron, 3rd Cavalry Regiment. The remaining personnel assigned to the HQ, AFV and HQ, ATF, also left when these commands were closed down in March. Some members of the Australian Army Training Team, Vietnam, remained until December when the AATTV was finally shut down after more than 10 years in Vietnam. The Australian Army Assistance Command, Vietnam, which came into existence in March, 1972, to provide training and other assistance to the Vietnamese left at the end of January, 1973.

During the 10 plus years Australians were committed to the war in Vietnam, 47,000 of them served there. 415 were killed in action and 2348 were wounded. Four Australians assigned to the AATTV won the Victoria Cross, the highest award for gallantry awarded by their country.

The Australians had rarely taken part in large operations during their time in Vietnam, but they had patrolled actively and had secured Phouc Tuy Province quite well. The Australians also used their long experience at jungle fighting to advantage, both in training ARVN units and in their own operations. The Australian and SAS troops were especially skilled at working with and leading indigenous units, functioning much as did the U.S. Special Forces in training local defense units, and many also served as advisors to ARVN Ranger units.

Uniforms and Equipment

Although the Australians used much U.S. equipment, they also had certain distinctive items of their own.

The standard headgear for the Aussies was the

'Digger' hat with wide brim turned up on the left side and regimental cap badge affixed at this point. This hat was normally worn by the Royal Australian Regiment and hence bore that formation's badge. The Digger hat, though often called olive drab, was lighter in color and at times appeared almost khaki. Black berets with 'Black Panther' beret badge or maroon berets with ARVN Ranger beret insignia were often worn by members of the Australian SAS assigned as advisors to ARVN Ranger Battalions or other special units such as the 1st ARVN Division's strike company. Although the Australian SAS wears a sand colored beret very similar to that worn by the British SAS it was rarely if ever seen in Vietnam. Australian armored crewmen sometimes wore black berets with the badge of the armored regiment. 'Boonie' or 'bush' hats in OD or camouflage were widely worn by the Australians as well. Some Aussies assigned to civic action projects, HQ, AFV, etc. might also be seen wearing the British style service hat with regimental badge on the front.

The basic Australian uniform was a set of utilities similar to those worn by U.S. troops. Like the slouch or Digger hat, the utilities are often called OD but in color photos usually appear lighter in hue. One notable difference in these utilities was that they had pockets located on the upper shirt sleeve. The trousers of these utilities were normally worn tucked into the combat boots, but not bloused. The Australians sometimes wore shorts, though not normally in the field. For non-line duty, a khaki or tan uniform consisting of shirt and trousers with stable belt or shirt and shorts with webbed belt was worn. Rank insignia was worn on shoulder tabs for officers and on the sleeve for enlisted personnel. Some Australian personnel – especially those in the SAS – wore tiger-striped camouflage utilities.

The basic Australian footgear was high topped black kangaroo hide combat boots similar in appearance to those in use with American troops, however, U.S. jungle boots were also widely used, especially as the war progressed.

During the early part of their involvement, Australian troops wore Australian pattern webbed gear, most easily identifiable by the two large magazine pouches worn on the belt over the hipbones. Canteens were worn at the back, and what from photos appears to be a knapsack was worn over the shoulder. Because the large magazine pouches were needed for the L1A1

rifle, many RAR troopers retained this gear until late in the war. The SAS, however, and other Aussie advisors to ARVN units used the U.S. M-56 harness with rucksacks. In some photos of SAS men with CIDG units, indigenous magazine pouches are worn. Equipment in use with other Australian units would often be a mix of Australian, British, and American.

In addition to regimental insignia which might be worn on the beret as in the case of armored crewmen, a curved metal AUSTRALIA tab was often worn on the shoulder loops and an insignia for the AATTV was sometimes worn on the sleeve. Since many of the SAS men serving in Vietnam were given warrant officers rank for easier dealings with U.S. and ARVN officers, it was relatively common to see the sleeve insignia bearing a crown worn by the WOs.

Light weapons in use by the Australians were for the most part the same as those used by the Americans. Exceptions – most notably the Browning Hi-Power 9 mm. auto pistol and L1A1 rifle – were normally the same as those in use with British forces. With the SAS and, later, other units, the M16 was widely used since it was substantially lighter than the L1A1, making it much easier to carry in the jungle. Some Sterling 9 mm. SMGs were also used by the Aussies, including the silenced Mk 5 (L34A1) version by the SAS. (The Centurion tank used by the Australians was considered by many to be the best armored fighting vehicle in Vietnam.)

New Zealand

The first Kiwis to serve in Vietnam arrived in July, 1964, when an engineer platoon and a surgical unit arrived 'in country'. Two years earlier, however, a 30 man detachment from the New Zealand SAS Squadron worked with the U.S. Marines and Army in Thailand performing road recon and training Thai personnel.

The first New Zealand combat unit sent to Vietnam was the 161st Battery RNZ Artillery which arrived in July, 1965. It was attached to the Australian Task Force serving with the 173rd Airborne Brigade. By the end of 1965, there were 119 New Zealanders serving in Vietnam.

In March, 1966, the artillery battery and surgical team were increased in strength, but by the end of 1966, only 155 New Zealand troops were in Vietnam.

1967, however, saw New Zealand increase its force considerably. In addition to more medical personnel, in May V Company, RNZ Infantry Regiment, arrived in Vietnam. It was followed in December by W Company and engineer and support troops. These two companies along with an Australian company formed an ANZAC battalion. Also arriving late in 1967 was No. 4 Troop, NZSAS, which was intended to provide long range patrol capability and to work with the Australian SAS in training civilian irregulars.

During 1968, New Zealand's troop strength in Vietnam changed little from 1967, dropping by 18 men. The NZSAS was especially active that year, mounting five man recon patrols and also setting ambushes along enemy trail networks. One officer and 25 other ranks made up the NZSAS troop.

During 1969, there was also little basic change in New Zealand's troop strength, though it did climb to 552 men, the peak during the war. Unlike the Australians, the New Zealanders did not rotate entire units in and out of Vietnam. Instead, they followed the U.S. practice of rotating men home and replacing them within the existing unit which remained in Vietnam. Except for the HQ, NZFV (New Zealand Forces, Vietnam), which was located in Saigon, virtually all New Zealand units were based at Nui Dat, Phuoc Tuy Province. As of June, 1969, combat units had the following strengths – 161st Battery – 131 men; V Company, RNZIR – 150 men; W Company, RNZIR – 150 men; and No. 4 Troop, NZSAS – 26 men. Other troops were in either support or administrative positions.

During 1968–70, the New Zealand forces were primarily involved in civic action programs, protection of the rice harvests, and patrolling within their area of responsibility. During 1970, New Zealand began reducing its forces 'in country' by withdrawing one infantry company (W Company). This withdrawal continued during 1971 when No. 4 Troop, NZSAS and 161st Artillery were pulled out in February and March, and V Company, RNZIR followed later in the year. Only a small advisory unit remained by the end of the year.

Uniforms and Equipment

The uniforms and equipment worn by the New Zealanders were very similar to that of the Australians, though the bush or boonie hat was commonly worn instead of the Australian 'Digger' hat. The New Zealand SAS wore camouflage utilities with camouflage bush hat. Because they frequently functioned as LRRPs, the NZSAS also adopted some of the same special equipment used by U.S. Army LRRPs. The M-16 was widely used among New Zealanders, especially the SAS.

Philippines

Sixteen Philippine Army officers arrived in Vietnam during August, 1964, to assist in pacification efforts at the local level. During 1965, the number of Philippine military personnel in Vietnam was increased to 72, most in civic action projects.

The major Philippine influx began, however, in the fall of 1966. The 1st Philippine Civic Action Group, Vietnam, arrived in Tay Ninh Province during September, 1966. As its name implies, this Philippine unit was primarily concerned with civic action projects and as a result had a large contingent of medical and engineering personnel assigned. There were, however, enough ground combat troops to provide security. The major units in 'PHILCAG' included an infantry battalion, a field artillery battery equipped with 105 mm. howitzers, a construction engineer battalion, a medical and dental battalion, a logistical support company, and an HQ and service company.

Surgical personnel were deployed at hospitals at My Tho (home base of the tough PRUs) and Phu Cuong and a rural medical team was at Bao Trai. Engineering personnel also began working shortly after their arrival on roads bordering the eastern side of Thanh Dien Forest. In December, Philippine engineering and security elements began clearing a resettlement site near the Thanh Dien forest. Philippine EOD (Explosive Ordnance Disposal) teams were especially useful in clearing the area of mines, booby traps, etc. By January, the VC were attacking Philippine work parties around the Thanh Dien area, and many firefights took place. The Philippine troops made it a point, however, to always operate within range of their 105s.

During 1967, Philippine strength dropped slightly to 2020 personnel in Vietnam. Some men were replaced when rotated back to the Philippines but no additional units were deployed. By early 1968, in fact, strength had dropped below 1800 since men returning home were not being replaced. In September-October, 1968, most of the troops who had completed two year tours in Vietnam were replaced.

In December, 1969, most of the remaining Philippine forces were pulled out, leaving just some support personnel and medical and dental teams. By March, 1970, only 131 personnel remained.

The Philippine troops had engaged in combat only to defend themselves, hence, their contribution was primarily to pacification of the area they served in through civic action programs.

Uniforms and Equipment

Most commonly worn Philippine headgear was a bush hat with the brim turned up on both sides. This hat was stiffer than the floppy bush hats commonly worn by U.S. or ARVN troops and almost resembled a USAF Air Commando hat or some of the hats of this type worn by French troops. After wear, however, this hat sometimes began to resemble the other types of bush hats. In fact, after a few months of wear in the boonies, a wide assortment of headgear began to look quite alike: they all became shapeless masses. The Philippine bush hat was not exactly OD in color, but had more brown in it, much like the brownish/green hue of some U.S. World War II uniforms. OD utility hats were also worn. The Philippine dress service hat was similar in appearance to that worn by the U.S. Army. For officers, it was blue and for enlisted men it was tan (slightly darker than khaki).

The standard field uniform was OD utilities similar to those worn by American troops. A tape was worn on the right breast reading PHILIPPINES and a name tape was worn on the left breast. Qualification badges such as airborne wings were sometimes worn on the left breast of the utilities, though an interesting photo exists of President Marcos visiting Philippine troops in Vietnam and wearing the small circular airborne insignia sometimes worn by American officers on their sidecaps on the turned up brim of his bush hat. Of course, as with General Westmoreland's airborne wings on his utility cap, presidents and four star generals can take a few liberties with the Uniform of the Day regulations. Rank insignia was worn on the collar for officers and on the sleeve for enlisted personnel. A white T-shirt was usually worn under the utility shirt. Some Philippine troops wore camouflage utilities (perhaps members of the Philippine Special Forces, a few of whom served in Vietnam) – normally tiger stripes – but the OD ones were standard. The dress uniform consisted of a tan, four pocket coat worn out over the trousers. A white shirt and black tie were worn under the coat. Officers or enlisted collar insignia were worn on the coat collars with branch insignia below for officers. Officers rank insignia were worn on the shoulders and enlisted personnel's rank insignia were worn on the sleeve.

Webbed gear and other equipment was basically U.S. pattern and as with other allied forces was updated to M-56 gear, plastic canteens, etc. as the equipment became available.

The highest ranking Philippine officer in Vietnam was normally a brigadier general who wore one silver five-pointed star. Colonels, lieutenant colonels, and majors wore respectively three, two, and one eight pointed gold stars which looked very much like stylized snowflakes. Captains, first lieutenants, and second lieutenants wore respectively three, two, and one silver triangles.

NCO rank was designated by a series of blue chevrons and bars on a khaki background. A master sergeant wore three chevrons and three bars with a capital 'M' in the middle, a first sergeant three chevrons and three bars with a capital 'F', a technical sergeant three chevrons and two bars, a staff sergeant three chevrons and one bar, a sergeant three chevrons, a corporal two chevrons, and a private first class one chevron. A private wore a blue triangle outlined in khaki meant to resemble the center portion of the normal NCO rank insignia but with all chevrons and bars deleted.

Early in their participation, Philippine troops were armed with M1 and M2 carbines and some M14s. Later, they were equipped with M16s. Colt 1911A1 autos were also widely used since many civic action units carried only sidearms for self-defense.

9 Communist Forces in the Indo-China and Vietnam Wars

In many ways Vietnamese Communism owes the U.S.A. the thanks for its survival. During World War II, arms were supplied to the Viet Minh through the OSS for use against the Japanese. Using these arms, the Viet Minh were able to seize Hanoi in August, 1945, upon the Japanese surrender. During the fight against Japan, as he would be for the next 30 years, Vo Nguyen Giap was the principal military planner for the Communists. British troops, re-armed Japanese prisoners of war, and French forces took action against Ho Chi Minh's supporters, however, and on 23 September, French troops stormed the Viet Minh headquarters in Saigon. This was, in effect, the beginning of the war between the Viet Minh and the French which lasted until 1954.

In the early stages of the war the Viet Minh avoided battle unless they greatly outnumbered the French forces. All the while, however, they were consolidating their power. Viet Minh military actions were limited to harassing the French to tie down their already inadequate manpower.

With the Communist victory in China, a ready source of arms to the north became available, and in 1950 the Viet Minh prepared to step up operations against the French. In preparation, General Giap raised, trained, and equipped three infantry divisions during 1950.

Giap began his offensive against the French by attacking isolated border outposts such as Dong Khe on the Chinese border. The Viet Minh deployed 14 infantry battalions and three artillery battalions against the French border forts, and before 1950 ended, the French had been driven out of the border regions, 6000 French soldiers having been lost along with thousands of weapons which the Viet Minh did not hesitate to turn against the French. By 1 January 1951, France had lost control of all of Vietnam to the north of the Red River.

By early 1951, the Viet Minh also had six full divisions ready for combat. The 304th, 308th, 312th, 316th, and 320th were 10,000 man infantry divisions; the 351st Heavy Division two artillery and one combat engineer regiments.

By January, 1951, in preparation for a push on Hanoi itself, the Communists deployed 81 battalions ready to strike. The first attack was against Vinh Yen. French Marshal de Lattre de Tassigny himself flew in to supervise the defense of Vinh Yen. On 16 January, Giap launched the 308th Viet Minh Division against the French in human wave attacks. Only French airpower and extensive use of napalm saved the French garrison. On the 17th, Giap sent the 312th Division in – once again using human wave attacks – but again the French fighter bombers dropped napalm and saved the French ground forces. The Viet Minh were finally forced to retreat, leaving 6000 dead and 500 prisoners. This was, indeed, a Viet Minh defeat, but the French were unable to follow it up by pursuing the retreating Communists, and the initiative remained with Giap who learned from his mistakes at Vinh Yen. The Viet Minh suffered two other defeats in 1951, at Mao Khe in March and along the Day River in June.

The French attempted to take the offensive in November, 1951, by occupying Hoa Binh, a Viet Minh staging area. Giap responded by attacking with his 304th, 308th, 312th, 316th, and 320th Divisions. First, the Viet Minh harassed the French supply lines. Road 6 was constantly cut. Once again, the Viet Minh used human wave tactics for the express purpose of inflicting as many casualties as possible on the French forces. The French eventually pulled their troops out in early January, 1952, giving the Viet Minh complete control of the west bank of the Black River except for one French bridgehead. Eventually, on 12 January 1952, the Viet Minh managed to close the river completely. The French were then forced to fight their way along Road 6 just to keep the Hoa Binh pocket supplied. Finally, beginning on 22 February, the French began retreating from Hoa Binh, suffering heavy losses along the way. The Viet Minh had suffered heavy losses themselves, but they had forced crack French units – paratroopers and Foreign Legionnaires – to retreat and had inflicted heavy casualties on the French. They had also scored a psychological victory by forcing the French to continue to give up ground.

Beginning in October, 1952, the Viet Minh launched another offensive with an attack against the French outpost at Nghia Lo which soon fell. The Viet Minh continued to push forward for more than a month with no French opposition. The 308th, 312th, and 316th Viet Minh Divisions were involved in this operation, the object of which was to gain control of the T'ai hill country in Northern Vietnam. After the fall of Nghai Lo on 17 October, the rest of the French outposts in the area were doomed. The French dropped paras ahead of the advancing Viet Minh, but they were surrounded at Tu Le. Seemingly, the Viet Minh had let the paras escape, but instead the 312th Division was waiting in ambush along the withdrawal route. Over three-fifths of them were lost.

While the Viet Minh were thrusting west, the French planned Operation 'Lorraine' to force the Viet Minh into a large battle. Giap knew exactly what the French planned but continued his drive into the T'ai country. To stop the French, he detached two regiments – the 36th and 176th – to act as a delaying force. The logistical problems faced by the French combined with the obvious successes of the Viet Minh forces caused Operation 'Lorraine' to be called off.

After 'Lorraine' the French kept hoping for a set piece battle in the field where they could annihilate the Viet Minh but Giap had learned Mao's precepts of guerrilla warfare too well.

Giap undertook no major offensives during early 1953 but deployed his divisions for an invasion of Laos which he began in April. French outposts held out as long as they could, but the French were forced into two defensive centers. Although Communist supply capability did not enable Giap to continue this drive he had established that the Viet Minh could move at will through territory west of the Black River, including Northern Laos, a psychological victory which helped sap the French will to fight.

The French avoided major actions during the next few months and so did the Viet Minh who slipped away when confronted by superior numbers. In November, 1953, though, the French dropped three parachute battalions to occupy Dien Bien Phu, which the Viet Minh had captured in November, 1952.

During much of 1953, also, the Viet Minh – through hit and run raids – eroded French mobility more and more. Just in North Vietnam,

80,000 French troops were tied down in the defense of 900 forts by less than 30,000 Viet Minh, and these were mostly regional peasant militiamen rather than regulars. The French were forced into a fortress mentality with Dien Bien Phu becoming the ultimate fortification. Although fighting continued for three months after its fall, Dien Bien Phu was decisive.

On 1 August 1954 the armistice became effective thus ending the Viet Minh's victorious battle against the French. Actually, the Viet Minh 421st Intelligence Battalion supported by other units continued to hunt for Frenchmen from the GCMA operating with guerrillas against the Communists long after the armistice.

After the Geneva Agreements had been reached and North and South Vietnam partitioned along the 17th Parallel, Viet Minh troops were called back to the North. However, Giap left a cadre of 1000 or more troops in the South as a basis for future guerrilla units. For the next couple of years, the People's Liberation Army was concerned mostly with consolidation of power in North Vietnam.

In 1957, however, the Communists began a new guerrilla war in South Vietnam. Joined by more than 1500 infiltrators from the North, the 1000 Viet Minh who had remained in the South began to recruit for the National Liberation Front of South Vietnam (the Viet Cong). They recruited primarily from religious dissidents and from the mountain tribes. By 1958, the Viet Cong felt strong enough to attack a prison to free Communist sympathizers and to ambush company sized government units. North Vietnam also gave aid and encouragement to the Pathet Lao (Laotian Communists) in order to keep its infiltration route – the Ho Chi Minh Trail – open to the South. On 21 October 1961, more than a thousand VC troops infiltrated the Kontum area and destroyed a string of South Vietnamese Army posts. Before 1961 ended, the Communists were in control of between one-half and two-thirds of the countryside in the Republic of Vietnam. Many of these gains were directly attributable to a campaign of terror against minor government officials such as village mayors, thousands of whom were executed by the VC. In September, 1961, the VC even captured the provincial capital of Phuoc Vinh, just 55 miles from Saigon. Capitalizing on their successes and the dissatisfaction with Diem's leadership, the VC had recruited 17,000 'troops' by late 1961. Because of stepped up U.S. aid to the South

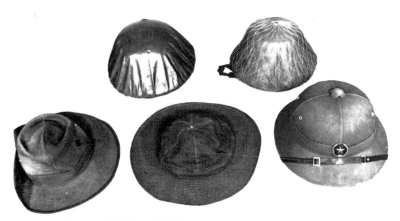

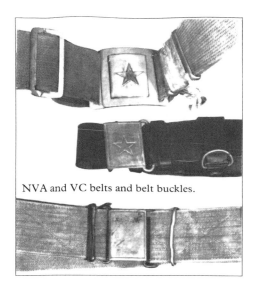

NVA and VC belts and belt buckles.

Selection of NVA and VC headgear.

Below center:
Front view of NVA regular's standard dark green uniform, a sun helmet with a gold five pointed star on red background insignia, and NVA jungle shoes. The weapon is the AK47 with F1N rifle grenade attached. The chest pouch holds three 30 round AK banana magazines.

Rear view of NVA regular's uniform. Note the NVA three pocket ruck sack with entrenching tool tucked into the top.

Front view of typical VC uniform: soft jungle hat, black pajamas, Ho Chi Minh sandals, SKS weapon and the Chicom style chest pouch for 200 rounds of ammo in stripper clips; across the shoulders is a black rice bag.

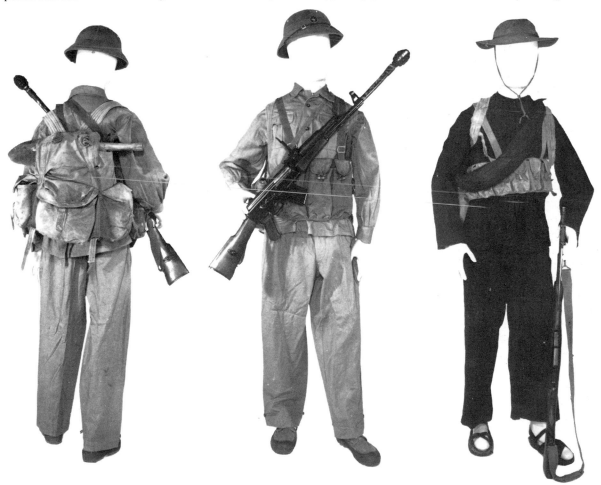

Vietnamese armed forces in early 1962, however, the VC found themselves in some difficulty, especially from the helicopters.

The VC 514th Battalion managed to gain an impressive victory in January, 1963, at Ap Bac, though, against strong ARVN forces with armor, helicopters, and U.S. advisors.

By 1963, the VC military forces could basically be classified into three categories. There were the local militia who undertook certain missions but then returned to their villages, the regional units who operated only in their home provinces, and the Main Force VC battalions – the 'Chu Loc' units. These Main Force battalions carried out the major operations. Main Force battalions usually had numerical designations between 502 and 634. By early 1964, four Main Force regiments were known to be operating in South Vietnam – the 108th, 120th, 126th, and 803rd.

During 1962–64 the VC also stepped up their attacks on rail lines, either by destroying bridges or tracks or by hijacking trains. Many roads were also mined to destroy convoys of trucks or armored vehicles. Also during 1964, raids against Saigon itself, especially against U.S. installations, were stepped up. Viet Cong sympathizers also encouraged the Buddhists in their demonstrations against the government.

On 5 August 1964, U.S. aircraft struck naval bases in North Vietnam as a result of the 'Gulf of Tonkin Incident'. After these air strikes the NVA strengthened its anti-aircraft defenses. Communist infiltration into South Vietnam was also stepped up after the air strikes.

By March, 1965, a full NVA division was operating in the Central Highlands of South Vietnam. In August, 1965, members of the 1st Viet Cong Regiment clashed with a U.S. Marine regiment in Quang Ngai Province taking heavy losses. Later in October, 1965, the first major clash between NVA and U.S. troops occurred at Plei Me where 6000 Communist troops including 2200 from the 33rd NVA Regiment attacked a Special Forces camp. The attack was driven off, and the NVA units were chased to the Cambodian border, eventually losing almost 1800 men. As was frequently the case, the NVA took refuge in Cambodia where it could rebuild its strength before going back into action. It should be noted that even severely mauled NVA or VC units were often regenerated resulting in the curious phenomenon of multiple regiments with the same numerical designation.

Although in 1966 the NVA and VC units suffered some heavy losses in actions against the heavily armed U.S. forces, they still remained a 'force in being'. This was especially true of the Viet Cong who just merged with the local population. Among Communist units heavily engaged in 1966 were the VC 9th Division and the NVA 324B Division. In all, 55,000 NVA/VC were killed during 1966. The Communists were undeterred, however, the losses being more than replaced by the 60,000 NVA troops entering South Vietnam during the year. By late 1966 NVA/VC combat strength was over 300,000.

In 1967, the NVA continued to increase its strength in the DMZ, especially in artillery. This artillery then used the 'haven' of the DMZ as a base from which to shell U.S. installations inside the Republic of Vietnam. In March, the NVA artillery stepped up its pounding of U.S. forward bases along the DMZ, firing more than 1000 rounds on 20 March. U.S. Marine and ARVN patrols out of Con Thien, Gio Linh, and Khe Sanh were also attacked by NVA units. The NVA also began occupying the hills overlooking Khe Sanh but were repulsed by the Marines after heavy fighting.

In early 1967 the NVA 610th Division was also involved in various actions against the 1st Air Cavalry in Binh Dinh Province. Other U.S. actions severely hampered Viet Cong operations in the Iron Triangle and forced the Communist HQ for South Vietnam to withdraw into Cambodia from Tay Ninh Province, psychologically a severe blow to the Communist cause.

VIET MINH AND NVA

Viet Minh Soldier This figure with his Chicom pattern quilted jacket shows the influence of the Chinese Communists upon the Viet Minh. His trousers are the black peasant 'pajamas'. His pith helmet has greenery tucked into the cover for camouflage, while additional camouflage is provided by the leaves around his neck. Such 'shawls' were re-furbished frequently so they did not turn brown. His weapon is the Chicom Type .50 SMG.
General Van Tien Dung This officer wears only a loose fitting green jacket – once again of Chinese Communist pattern – and trousers. His footgear is a pair of captured French patrol boots. His headgear is a reed sun helmet with green cover, bearing the circular cap badge sometimes worn by Communist forces. **NVA Regular Infantryman** This regular North Vietnamese infantryman wears the standard green NVA utility uniform with webbed belt whose aluminium buckle bears the red star. He wears standard NVA jungle shoes of canvas and rubber (patterned on the French patrol boot). The sun helmet with plastic cap badge was widely standardized among NVA regulars. His weapon is the Chicom Type 56 (AK47), for which he wears the well-known chest pouch for three 'banana' clips.

VIET MINH AND NVA

Viet Minh Soldier

General van Tien Dung

NVA Regular Infantryman

1967 ended with more border attacks. Around Dak To, the NVA attacked border outposts, and probed towards Khe Sanh and also trying to draw American strength away from the cities in preparation for the Tet Offensive. Two NVA divisions were also massed near Khe Sanh in anticipation of what the North Vietnamese hoped would be the U.S. Dien Bien Phu, though Giap was certainly astute enough to realize that U.S. air power would make a victory such as Dien Bien Phu difficult if not impossible. Infiltration into the South was also stepped up in preparation for the Tet offensive. By the end of 1967, the NVA/VC had more than 60,000 combatants within South Vietnam.

Tet was to be the main Communist offensive to conquer large parts of Vietnam and combined with an American defeat at Khe Sanh would, felt many of the North's leaders, result in a quick and victorious conclusion to the war. One important leader, however, did not concur. General Giap felt that the Tet Offensive was too much of a gamble and did not follow the precepts of guerrilla warfare. To some extent, the North Vietnamese seemed to have fallen prey to their own propaganda and were counting on a general uprising in the South in support of them when they struck. Although they captured some provincial capitals, Tet turned out to be a disaster for the Viet Cong, more than half of the 80,000 men involved in the offensive being killed. Ironically, a small operation by a suicide squad which achieved only limited success against the U.S. Embassy was blown out of proportion in the press in the U.S.A. and gave the Viet Cong a propaganda victory if not a military one.

The other major NVA/VC operation of early 1968 was the siege of Khe Sanh. The battle for that Marine base began on 21 January 1968. Among the NVA divisions involved in the siege were the 304th and 325th Infantry Divisions. The 320th and 324th Divisions were nearby and could reinforce the besiegers as needed. Khe Sanh held and was relieved on 14 April.

For the remainder of 1968, the Communist forces reverted primarily to harassment raids while trying to recover from the heavy losses suffered during Tet and at Khe Sanh. During 1969, the North Vietnamese became conservative both because of the heavy losses suffered in 1968 and because as the U.S.A. began the process of 'Vietnamization' the Communists realized that by biding their time they would not have to contend with American firepower.

During 1969 the NVA/VC attacked less often while waiting for the U.S. troops to leave. Still, 115,000 more soldiers infiltrated into the South to make up for the losses suffered during Tet. Forces in South Vietnam or just across the border in Laos, Cambodia, or North Vietnam numbered 250,000 – 100,000 of which were NVA regulars.

Once again in 1970 the Viet Cong avoided large scale action and limited themselves to rocket or mortar attacks, booby traps, and small ambushes. There was a relatively large attack by up to 3000 Communist troops against the Special Forces camp at Dak Seang in April, but it was unsuccessful. The VC and NVA also continued their operations from just across the border in Cambodia, and this prompted the U.S.A. to become interested in attacking the Communists in their 'sanctuaries'. The Communists in Cambodia – both Vietnamese and Cambodian – also became involved in a full scale war with Cambodian government forces in 1970. At the end of April, U.S. and ARVN troops moved into Cambodia to strike at NVA/VC supply lines. The Communists, however, had known of the attacks in advance and had retreated further into Cambodia. Because they had infiltrated the South Vietnamese army and Civil Service thoroughly, the Communists had a rather effective intelligence apparatus. Thus any large operation such as the one into Cambodia was compromised before it began. Reaction in the States to the American incursion was such that the Communists actually benefitted from the attack as pressure on the President to withdraw American troops from Southeast Asia grew even stronger. 1970 also saw the Khmer Rouge – Cambodian Communists – along with NVA and VC units winning the war for Cambodia against government troops. Only American air power was staving off defeat for the Lon Nol regime.

Communist troops were also present in Laos in large numbers – up to 100,000 NVA troops at some times. The local Communists – the Pathet Lao – also were waging a guerrilla war against the Laotian government troops. In 1970, the NVA 70B Corps was activated in the Laotian Panhandle. Consisting of three infantry divisions (304th, 308th, 320th), two artillery regiments, and one armored regiment, this force was poised to strike into Cambodia or South Vietnam.

To contain this threat, South Vietnamese troops moved into Laos in February, 1971, with U.S. air support. Elements of three NVA divi-

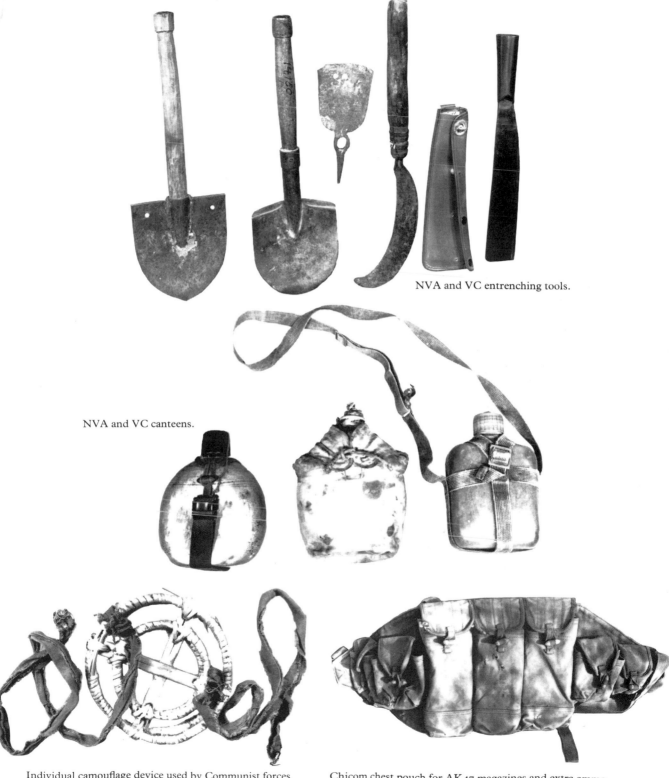

NVA and VC entrenching tools.

NVA and VC canteens.

Individual camouflage device used by Communist forces throughout the Indo-China and Vietnam Wars.

Chicom chest pouch for AK47 magazines and extra ammo.

sions hit the ARVNs, inflicting heavy casualties on the crack South Vietnamese Rangers and paratroopers spearheading the drive. The Communists, however, also took heavy losses, especially from American air strikes.

By 10 March, the ARVN units were withdrawing. They had succeeded in disrupting Communist plans for an offensive, but both sides had suffered heavy casualties. The Ho Chi Minh Trail which had been cut for a few days was operational again almost immediately, and supplies continued to flow southward to Communist forces. Also, the three best ARVN divisions had been decimated.

In early 1971, the NVA and Pathet Lao began to push Meo troops under Vang Pao out of the Laotian highlands. It looked as if Cambodia and Laos would be Communist controlled.

As the Americans were pulled out, plans were made in the North for a full scale invasion of the South. Although troops had been infiltrated in increasing numbers during early 1972, and divisional sized units including armor were poised to strike south, the actual invasion did not begin until the end of March, 1972.

At least four NVA divisions, including the 324B Division, were thrown against ARVN forward support bases in I Corps. These NVA units were the most heavily armed ever to enter the South. T-34, T-54, and PT-76 tanks along with SA-2 and SA-7 missiles and 130 mm. guns were all included in the armament of the attacking NVA. By 1 May, ARVN units had been driven back to the Tach Me River. Other NVA units were thrusting into South Vietnam from Laos and Cambodia in an attempt to cut the country into pieces. In I Corps, Quang Tri City was abandoned to the attackers and Hue was threatened, while attackers drove towards An Loc and Tay Ninh in III Corps and Kontum in II Corps. Two VC and one NVA divisions were thrusting towards An Loc with Saigon as their ultimate objective. After initially retreating, the ARVNs had rallied, but the presence of U.S. advisors and U.S. air power had still played the decisive role. By mid-June, the attacks on An Hog and Kontum had been repulsed and by September Quang Tri City had been recaptured.

The NVA and VC had retreated from the urban areas, but as of late 1972, there were more than 140,000 front line Communist troops in Vietnam, and they still controlled a lot of territory. Twelve NVA Divisions – the 1st, 2nd, 3rd, 7th, 304th, 308th, 312th, 320th, 320B, 324B,

325th, and 711th – were known to be 'in country' along with two VC divisions – the 5th and 9th. Additionally, there were many independent regimental sized units, including four artillery regiments. Obviously, though repulsed, the Communists were not defeated.

Even after the Paris 'Peace' Agreement, the Communists continued to infiltrate more troops into South Vietnam, by 1974 controlling up to one-third of the country and maintaining 145,000 troops in the South. They also had built roadways specifically for troop and supply movement into the South. Even Khe Sanh was controlled by the NVA and had been converted into a Communist airfield. Making things even easier for the Communists, U.S. aid had been curtailed, meaning South Vietnam would be even less capable of countering the Communist threat. Cambodia was in even worse shape. From 1973 through early 1975, the Khmer Rouge had been tightening their noose around Phnom Penh, the Cambodian capital which fell in April 1975.

By 1974, the North Vietnamese were ready for a final drive into South Vietnam. Some 300,000 troops were either 'in country' or poised on the borders. The only question was when would they strike? Realizing the South's greatest strength was its air power, the Communists had 23 AA regiments and one SAM regiment ready to move in with the invasion forces. Originally, the Communist war plan called for widespread attacks in 1975 with the major offensive in 1976.

In January, 1975, with the NVA 9th Division threatening Saigon to tie down troops, attacks were launched against Phuoc Long. By March, North Vietnamese forces under the command of Gen. Van Tien Dung were ready to drive on the

---

VIET CONG

Female Assassin She wears typical peasant garb but is armed with the Chicom Type 64 silenced assassination weapon. **Frogman** The VC used many frogmen in attempts to plant limpet mines on U.S. ships. Although many used no SCUBA equipment, those who did usually had a mixture of Warsaw Pact and French military SCUBA gear with some civilian items thrown in. This swimmer wears Soviet air tanks, North Vietnamese rubber helmet, and possibly some French equipment. **Irregular** This VC wears French style jungle hat, black 'Pajamas', and Ho Chi Minh sandals made of truck tires and old inner tubes. He carries up to a month's supply of rice in the tubular rice bag worn across his chest. His canvas gear is homemade and includes a haversack, grenade pouch, and ammo pouches. His rifle is the French MAS36, thousands of which were captured during the Indo-China War. He also carries a punji stake, whose points have been fire hardened.

VIET CONG

Female Assassin

Frogman

Irregular

important city of Ban Me Thuot. NVA tanks entered the city on 11 March 1975. ARVN troops were also forced to withdraw from Kontum and Pleiku. Hue, DaNang, Nha Trang and Cam Ranh Bay had fallen by the first week in April.

Seizing the opportunity, the North Vietnamese revised their strategy and decided to drive for Saigon and victory. By 29 April, Communist 130 mm. guns were emplaced around Saigon and were shelling Tan Son Nhut. On 30 April, the South Vietnamese surrendered. By December, 1975 Laos was also under Communist control.

This victory did not bring peace, however. The Vietnamese were already looking westward at Kampuchea (formerly Cambodia). Beginning late in 1977, Vietnamese troops under Gen. Tran Van Tra attacked Kampuchea in force using captured U.S. equipment as well as their Chinese and Soviet made weapons. The drive continued through the first part of 1978. Vietnamese troops were also moved into Laos in large numbers during 1978. At this time, the Vietnamese Army was one of the largest in the world. It was composed of 25 infantry divisions, 45 artillery regiments, 60 air defense regiments, and 30 tank battalions. Using 12 of these divisions, the Vietnamese completed the conquest of Kampuchea by mid-January, 1979.

As a result of the Kampuchean invasion and the mistreatment of ethnic Chinese in Vietnam, the People's Republic of China invaded Vietnam on 17 February 1979. Vietnamese militiamen harassed the Chinese invaders, while regular units of the Vietnamese People's Army were rushed northwards. The VPA fought well against the Chinese – their years of combat experience standing them in good stead – but the Chinese withdrew on their own after their 'show of force'.

Vietnam still maintains a massive army numbering over 600,000, which absorbs 50 per cent. of the country's gross national product.

Uniforms and Equipment

During the period right after World War II, the Viet Minh forces were dressed much like the peasantry they sprang from. Black 'pajamas' were commonly worn along with the palm leaf hat. Some captured Japanese uniforms and headgear, including helmets, were also used. By the late 1940s and early 1950s, however, the Viet Minh had begun to receive aid from China. Among regular Viet Minh divisions beginning in about 1950, woven reed pith helmets and a green uniform consisting of shirt and trousers began to be standardized. Webbed gear was Japanese or French, or U.S. gear left over from World War II OSS drops or, more likely, captured in Korea. In fact, large supplies of U.S. weapons and equipment were given to the Viet Minh by the Chinese who had captured them from the Nationalists or in Korea. At least some German equipment was also used, captured by the Russians during World War II.

Because of French air power and the Communist reliance on ambushes, the Viet Minh were very camouflage conscious, and their palm leaf helmets were usually equipped with camouflage nets. Normally, each Viet Minh regular also carried a wire mesh camouflage disk to which he would attach local flora.

As already stated, the Viet Minh received some U.S. equipment from the Chinese. Especially useful were M1 Garands and M1 or M2 carbines since ammunition for them could be captured from the French. Captured French MAT49 SMGs and 7.5 mm. MAS bolt action rifles were also widely used. Other weapons encountered with the Viet Minh included Japanese Type 38 and 99 rifles, German MP38/40 SMGs, Soviet Moisin-Nagant 1891/30 7.62 mm. rifles, and Soviet PPSh 41 SMGs.

After the French withdrawal, the equipment of the People's Liberation Army or NVA (North Vietnamese Army) became even more standardized, though militia units or VC units in the South continued to have a wide assortment of 'uniforms', weapons and equipment.

Best known headgear worn by the NVA, and to a lesser extent by Main Force Viet Cong units, was the sun helmet. Many of these were manufactured in North Vietnam of pressed paper and had green cloth covers which were not removable since they were bonded on. Similar white helmets were also occasionally seen, but it is possible that these were just examples without the cover. These helmets came in one size with a simple adjustable head band and a leather chin strap. True pith helmets were also worn, once again with green cloth covers.

Seen in use with the NVA – primarily in the early days of the war – and also with Main Force Viet Cong was the plastic sun helmet manufactured in China. This helmet had the appearance of a truncated cone and was also manufactured of woven reeds during the 1950s for use by NVA units.

Jungle workshop copy of the Thompson SMG.

Although the VC were armed more frequently with Chicom or Sovblok weapons as the war progressed, locally produced ordnance such as these crude VC grenades were still encountered.

Jungle workshop automatic pistols used by the VC. The pistol at left is a rough copy of the Colt 1911 and/or French M1935A.

SKS rifle (Chicom Type 56 Carbine).

Chicom Type 56 (AK47) assault rifle widely used by the NVA and VC.

153

MiG-21に乗りこもうと
北ベトナムのパイロッ

North Vietnam Air Force MiG-21 pilot.

Below:
North Vietnam Army staff officers from Hanoi.

Opposite:
North Vietnam Air Force fighter pilot at left with MiG-21.

Any of these sun or pith helmets might be worn with a circular metal or plastic badge having a five pointed star on a red background surrounded by a gold rice stalk wreath which some authorities say indicated officers rank, but this is not certain.

Two types of soft caps were worn by the NVA. One was a dark green field cap with a sun flap and ear flaps. The other was very similar in appearance to those worn by the Communist Chinese Army. Most were greenish tan in color, though the Khmer Rouge and Pathet Lao both affected similar hats in green. Either of these hats might be worn with a red star on the front.

Also widely used among the NVA and VC was the floppy NVA jungle hat in tan, green, dark blue, or black. This hat bore quite a resemblance to the French issue jungle hat and may have been based on it. These floppy hats were well suited to the jungle and were Communist equivalents of the U.S. 'boonie' or Australian 'digger' hats.

Finally, French, Soviet, Chinese, and other helmets occasionally were used by NVA troops,

most commonly AA crewmen. Tank crews also wore padded Warsaw Pact style helmets. Rarely encountered and rumored to be reserved for elite assault troops were blue berets of Eastern European origin. Whatever headgear was worn, though, NVA and VC Main Force usually had 'white sidewalls' (i.e. no hair right above the ears or low on the neck).

The standard NVA uniform was basic to the point of being spartan. It consisted of a green cotton shirt and trousers. The shirt had long sleeves and two button down pockets, one on each breast. The buttons were of green plastic. Trousers normally had three pockets and could be gathered at the ankles by buttoning them. Khaki, blue, and brown NVA uniforms were also occasionally encountered, though the latter three were rarely seen. There was also a dress uniform sometimes encountered of brown or tan material with a long sleeved jacket having four pockets. This jacket was worn outside the trousers. This uniform appeared similar to some Soviet uniforms and was worn with a hat of Soviet pattern. This was also one of the few NVA uniforms on which rank/and or branch insignia were worn.

Dark blue sweaters were rarely encountered in wear and like the blue berets previously mentioned were reportedly issued to elite troops. Under their uniforms NVA troops normally wore a dark green loin cloth.

The VC being basically a peasant army wore the black 'pajamas' of the peasants. Some of these shirts were collarless pullover types, while others had buttons and pockets. Either full length black trousers or black shorts were normally worn. Main Force VC units also wore a tan uniform. Some say this uniform was for use by both NVA and VC units operating in Laos.

One type of NVA footwear was the green or tan canvas shoe which was similar to U.S. high top tennis shoes but most closely resembled the French lightweight jungle or patrol boot. Normally, these shoes had brown rubber lug soles. For wear with the brown dress uniform, low dress shoes of Soviet pattern were available to higher ranking officers. The most commonly encountered shoe among NVA and VC fighters, however, was the ubiquitous Ho Chi Minh sandal with soles made from old truck tires. Many VC and even NVA troops fought barefoot.

NVA/VC belts were either of cotton or of nylon webbing salvaged from captured U.S. equipment. The buckles were either plain or bore a five pointed star. Both buckles were probably of Chinese origin, and those having a star were supposedly issued to VC or NVA officers. Some belts of a reddish brown plastic material were also worn, many having a plain buckle patterned after those on U.S. issue belts but probably hand made.

Perhaps no piece of NVA/VC equipment offers such diversity as the assortment of pouches or other load carrying gear. No doubt the most widely recognized piece of gear was the Chicom (or NVA copies thereof) chest pouch which had three pockets for AK47 'banana' magazines and four smaller pockets – two on each side – for cleaning kit and boxes of extra ammunition. Plastic or wood toggles were normally used as fasteners on these pouches which were made of heavy green cotton or canvas. There were, however, many variations in the types of ammunition pouches used. Another type of AK47 pouch was made of green cotton and was meant to be worn either by use of a shoulder strap or with belt loops on its reverse side. The interior was divided into five compartments, each of which held one 30 round AK47 magazine. There was also a long narrow pocket for an AK cleaning kit and one on the opposite side for an oiler. One flap secured by a strap and buckle covered the main compartment.

Another widely used ammunition pouch was the 10 pocket type for the SKS which had shoulder straps and was worn at the waist. Also of heavy green cotton or canvas, this pouch used wooden toggle buttons. The shoulder straps were crossed at the back. Two 10 round stripper clips were carried in each pocket, giving a capacity of 200 rounds.

Other ammunition pouches included green ones of Chinese origin for the Moisin-Nagant rifle. These were 10 pocket chest pouches. Also sometimes seen in wear were bandoliers for SKS, French MAS, or Moisin-Nagant ammunition. These bandoliers or other locally produced ammunition pouches could be of 'black pajama' material or of any other cloth or canvas available. Frequently, salvaged U.S. snap fasteners were used on the flaps of these pouches. Captured U.S. magazine pouches were used when available.

Pouches to carry drum magazines for the Chicom type 56 LMG (the Soviet RPD) were also sometimes worn by machine-gunners. These pouches were normally of green canvas and used a shoulder strap.

In fairly wide use among NVA units were an assortment of grenade pouches. The best known type was probably the Chicom four pocket one worn on the belt but which also had shoulder straps. Because the NVA and VC used a large variety of grenades, pouches came in many different shapes. Most commonly, however, they were for the stick fragmentation grenade. Other two pocket pouches of green canvas were used for stick grenades, a tie strap being used to secure the grenades, only the fragmentation heads of which fitted into the pouches. Crudely made leather grenade pouches were also sometimes used.

The most common NVA rucksack was a Chicom type with three external pockets. Two adjustable shoulder straps were attached to the main body of this ruck which was made of dark green canvas or cotton. Side pockets were secured by ties, while the larger center pocket was covered with a flap having a buckle and strap. There was also a version having only two external pockets, and assorted handmade or captured rucksacks as well as some of Czech origin might also be worn. Eastern European knapsacks, especially of Czech manufacture, were occasionally used by both the NVA and VC.

Not exactly a rucksack or knapsack but widely used was the tubular cloth rice bag worn over the shoulder. These bags came in different colors, usually black or white, and held up to a month's supply of rice. The appearance of this piece of equipment was such that it has sometimes erroneously been called a bedroll.

Among canteens used by the NVA/VC, the aluminum Chinese one painted olive green and fitted with cotton straps for carrying over the shoulder was most common. These same canteens were also issued with green cotton or canvas covers having loops so that they could be worn on the belt. There were also some green molded plastic canteens which used green canvas covers meant to be worn on the belt. Rarely encountered but occasionally used were black rubberized bladder canteens or water bags.

In addition to other equipment, the NVA regular or Viet Cong might carry attached to the rucksack or other gear the individual camouflage device made from rings of bamboo, reeds, wire, etc. and meant to be attached to the helmet or some other piece of equipment with twigs or branches interwoven through it to reduce chances of detection from the air when moving through the jungle. This device changed little from the time the Viet Minh started using it.

Knives, machetes, and other edged implements in use with the NVA/VC tended to be quite rough in manufacture. Old files or other pieces of steel were used for the blades, and handles were made of wood, bamboo, or just cord wrapped around the tang. VC entrenching tools were as rudimentary as their knives, usually having a hand forged pick or shovel head and a bamboo handle. NVA entrenching tools were somewhat more standardized and consisted of a steel shovel blade with wooden handle, the whole implement being about 20 inches long.

Although virtually never worn in the combat zone, the NVA did have a system of rank and branch insignia worn on shoulder boards or collar. Shoulder boards for NCOs normally had a blue background with red border. One stripe designated a corporal, two stripes a sergeant, and three stripes a master sergeant. Officers shoulder boards were normally yellow with a red border. A third lieutenant had one stripe, a second lieutenant one stripe and one star, and a first lieutenant one stripe and two stars. A captain had one stripe and three stars, a senior captain one stripe and

four stars, a major two stripes and one star, a lieutenant colonel two stripes and two stars, a colonel two stripes and three stars, and a senior colonel two stripes and four stars. Generals shoulder boards bore no stripes, but one, two, three, and four gold stars respectively for brigadier general, major general, lieutenant general, and general. In some color photographs generals stars appear to be green rather than gold, perhaps determined by the uniform being worn.

Collar insignia consisted of red parallelograms. Officers wore plain red ones, while generals were also plain but were smaller. A student officer had a yellow stripe in the middle of his insignia. A master sergeant bore a yellow stripe and three stars, a sergeant a yellow stripe and two stars, and a corporal a yellow stripe with one star. A private first class had two stars and no stripe and a private second class one star with no stripe. Collar insignia of the same shape and color bearing branch insignia or branch insignia and rank were also worn. Among those branches for which there were insignia were – cavalry: crossed sabers with horseshoe; band: hunting horn and drumstick; chemical: retort; ordnance: crossed rifles; engineer: crossed pick and shovel; artillery: crossed guns; armor: a tank; medical: a red cross on white circle.

Although by the later stages of the Vietnam War, a certain level of weapons standardization had been reached by the NVA and even VC units, there was still far more diversity than among U.S. or ARVN forces. If any weapon can be said to have been standardized, it was the AK47 assault rifle in one of its many guises. Soviet, Chinese, and Czech (the Model 58) versions of the AK were all encountered in quantity.

The Soviet SKS or Chicom Type 56 semi-automatic rifle was also widely used by the NVA and later by the Viet Cong. Other rifles used to greater or lesser degrees were the U.S. M16, M1 or M2 Carbine, and M1 Garand; French MAS36; Soviet M1940 Moisin-Nagant or M1944 Carbine (the Chinese Type 53), M1891/30 rifle; and German KAR-98K (via East Germany and the Soviet Bloc).

After the AK47 and SKS perhaps the most widely used weapons were an assortment of sub-machine-guns. The NVA K50 was a North Vietnamese amalgamation of design features of the PPSh41, Chicom Type 50, and French MAT49. MAT49s and VC home workshop conversions of the design chambered for the 7.62 mm. Soviet round were also popular. Soviet

PPSh41 and PPS SMGs received some use, mostly in the earlier stages of the war, but with North Vietnamese or VC militia units might still turn up into the 1970s. German MP38/40s, Indonesian Beretta Model 12s, U.S. M3A1s (or the Chinese Nationalist Type 36 copy), and jungle workshop copies of the Thompson SMG or other designs were all used to some extent.

Normally, only fairly high ranking officers or Viet Cong sent on assassination missions carried handguns, but some were used by Communist forces. The French M1935-A, Soviet Makarov (PM), and Soviet Tokarev TT33 were probably the most common weapons. Others in use included Japanese Model 14 Nambus, Czech M1950s, German Walther P38s, German Mauser M1896s (also Chinese copies of this weapon), and copies of the U.S. 1911A1 and Belgium Browning Hi-Power which were fabricated in jungle workshops and chambered for either the 7.62 mm. or 9X18 mm. Soviet pistol round. Finally, some VC assassins were armed with the Chicom Type 64 7.65 mm. silenced pistol. This weapon had an integral silencer and a slide lock to eliminate functioning noise and was specifically designed for political murders.

As with other weapons, just about any light machine-gun they could acquire was used by the Viet Cong, but the NVA were somewhat standardized on the Chicom Type 53 or its Soviet counterpart, the DP or DPM. The Soviet RPD or its Chinese versions the Type 56 was also used along with the Chinese Type 58 version of the Soviet RP46. In later years, the Soviet RPK, the light machine-gun version of the AK became popular. Among VC units, any of those LMGs mentioned above might be encountered as might the French M1924/29, Japanese Type 96, Czech ZB26 (usually the Chicom Type 26 version), Chicom copies of the Danish Madsen, and U.S. M60 GPMGs or 1919 MGs.

The principal NVA/VC anti-tank weapon was the NVA/VC Model B40, also known as the Chicom AT launcher No. 56 or the Soviet RPG-2. Some NVA units were later equipped with the newer RPG7 launcher. Other such weapons included the Chicom launcher No. 51, copies of the U.S. M20 Bazooka, and the Czech P27.

Mortars used included the Chicom Type 63 (a copy of the U.S. 60 mm.), French M35, Chicom Type 53 (copy of the Soviet M1937), Chicom 60 mm. 'knee mortar' (copy of the World War II Japanese model), and the Chicom copy of the French M44 or U.S. M1 81 mm. mortar. It was a fairly standard Communist practice to actually use 82 mm. mortars so that captured U.S. or ARVN mortar bombs could be used in their weapons but captured Communist mortar bombs could not be used in 81 mm. mortars. Early rocket attacks were carried out using the Soviet 122 mm. tripod launched rocket which weighed 112 lbs (51 kg.), 42 lbs (19 kg.) of which was warhead. This rocket had a range of up to 10 miles. The 122 mm. was superseded in 1968 by the Chinese 107 mm. rocket which retained the range and effectiveness of the 122 mm. but was lighter and, hence, more manportable.

Many VC grenades were made in jungle workshops and were crude copies of U.S., Japanese, or Soviet designs. Also used by the NVA or VC, though, were the Chicom Type 1/M33 (Soviet F-1), Chicom PWP (a white phosphorus grenade), Chinese M32 (Soviet RGD-5), Soviet RG42, Soviet RGD33, and Soviet RPG6, RGP40, and RPG43 anti-tank grenades.

North Vietnamese pilots wore flight suits of Soviet pattern with the distinctive Soviet white pilots helmet which framed the face completely, a portion passing under the chin. This helmet also had a tinted visor. Ground personnel wore the normal green NVA uniform and cotton field cap. The Air Force cap insignia was similar to the Army's, but the star was superimposed over wings.

The standard North Vietnamese sailors uniform consisted of dark blue sailor shirt with white sailors collar and a blue and white striped t-shirt visible at the neck. Trousers were similar in pattern to those worn by the NVA. A patrol hat was worn with a hat badge similar to the Army's but bearing a star superimposed on an anchor.

Although strictly speaking Viet Cong frogmen were not part of the North Vietnamese Navy, this is a convenient place to discuss them. VC frogmen launched hundreds of attacks on American or South Vietnamese ships or bridges, sinking a few ships with limpet mines or homemade '4-4-4' mines. There were other homemade types of VC mine which were also used. Many VC frogmen swam under water without scuba gear, but in a few cases equipment was available. A common assemblage might include Soviet air tanks, a North Vietnamese rubberized helmet, and French face mask. Often, this improvised scuba gear was obtained from commercial sources outside of North Vietnam. Although VC combat swimmers gained some successes, for the most part they were countered effectively by American security measures, notably US killer dolphins.

Index

Numbers in *italic* refer to black and white illustrations. Numbers in **bold** refer to colour illustrations.